D0564348

GARDENING
WITH
herbs

GARDENING
WITH
herbs

Emelie Tolley and Chris Mead

Design by Stark Design

Clarkson Potter/Publishers • New York

Also by Emelie Tolley and Chris Mead

HERBS
COOKING WITH HERBS
GIFTS FROM THE HERB GARDEN
THE HERBAL PANTRY
A POTPOURRI OF PANSIES

Text copyright © 1995 by Emelie Tolley

Photographs copyright © 1995 by Chris Mead

All rights reserved. No part of this book may be reproduced or transmitted in any form or by any
means, electronic or mechanical, including photocopying, recording, or by an information storage and retrieval system,
without permission in writing from the publisher.

Published by Clarkson N. Potter, Inc., 201 East 50th Street, New York, New York 10022.

Member of the Crown Publishing Group.

Random House, Inc. New York, Toronto, London, Sydney, Auckland

CLARKSON N. POTTER, POTTER, and colophon are trademarks of Clarkson N. Potter, Inc.

Manufactured in China

Library of Congress Cataloging-in-Publication Data
Tolley, Emelie.
Gardening with herbs / Emelie Tolley and Chris Mead.—1st ed. p. cm.
Includes index.
1. Herb gardening. 2. Landscape gardening. 3. Herb gardening—Pictorial works.
4. Landscape gardening—Pictoral works. I. Mead, Chris. II. Title.
SB351.H5T64 1995 712—dc20 94-23825 CIP

ISBN 0-517-58332-1

10 9 8 7 6 5 4 3 2 1

First Edition

To my sister, Myra, whose love of gardening inspired me.—E.T.

To Emelie, for her great research and writing, which have made our books so

successful, and for conceiving herbs as a lifestyle.—C.M.

Acknowledgments

So many people have contributed their knowledge and goodwill to this book over the more than five years we have been working on it, there is no way we can thank each of them individually here. We have been continually touched with the generosity of those who have allowed us to visit their gardens and shared with us their thoughts, their gardening skills, and the whereabouts of their favorite gardens. While not all of the gardens we visited appear in the following pages, the friendship and knowledge we accumulated have helped shape the book and so we say a deeply felt thank you to each of you.

Special thanks go, too, to several dear friends without whose help in finding and scheduling our trips to distant places our task would have been impossible: Alan and

Dorothy Jones and Margery and Edward Dines in England; Jacqueline Horscher-Thomas and Christopher Petkanus in France; Dulcey Mahar in Oregon; Linda Veffer in Ohio; Audrey Julian in Pennsylvania; and Jimmie Cramer in Maryland.

And, of course, we are always grateful to all our friends and colleagues at Clarkson Potter who shepherd our work through the endless process of bookmaking and bookselling, but most especially our editor, Pam Krauss, and her able assistant, Anne Tamsberg; Lauren Shakely; Howard Klein and Jane Treuhaft; and Adriane Stark, whose handsome design enhanced our material for your eyes.

Contents

Introduction

Gardening with herbs is delightful. Strolling through the garden early in the morning while drops of dew still nestle in the pleated leaves of a lady's mantle plant, walking along a lavender-lined path at high noon, enveloped in the heady fragrance released by the heat

ABOVE: A chubby standard marks a corner of Anne Cox Chambers's French potager. OPPOSITE: The herb garden at Fort Vancouver.

of the sun, or simply nibbling a refreshing mint leaf while weeding on a hot day are just a few of the satisfactions enjoyed by those who grow herbs.

When Chris and I started work on our first book, *Herbs: Gardens, Decorations, and Recipes,* twelve years ago, many people were just beginning to discover how rewarding these plants could be. They were starting to grow herbs in a separate little herb garden, to turn the dried flowers and leaves into fragrant potpourris and beautiful wreaths, and to enliven foods with the pungent leaves or colorful flowers of fresh herbs. Since then, many thousands more have come under the spell of these enchanting plants, and knowledge of how to use them as decorations and in the kitchen has grown immeasurably. Now, our percep-

tions of gardening with herbs is changing as we realize that herbs needn't be

confined to their own special spot: the potential for enjoying their beauty and

fragrance goes far beyond the traditional herb garden. This is especially good

news for those short on space. As an alternative they might tuck a few fra-

grant plants into borders and rock gardens, use herbs as ground cover, add

Herbs line the narrow brick path in Mary Flegle's kitchen garden.

their variety to a shade garden, train them into a hedge or over an arbor or wall, or plant them in containers.

In the broadest sense, herbs encompass a far greater range of plants than the obvious culinary

favorites. Years ago there was little distinction between the herbs and flowers in monastery and cottage gar-

dens: all were grown because they were useful. Pungent thyme and sage, for example, were prized for their

antiseptic qualities as well as for their zesty flavor. Such garden favorites as foxglove (digitalis), feverfew,

mallow, and peonies were trusted medical remedies; roses, lavender, and pinks were a source of fragrance

for the house and its mistress. In fact, many plants we now think of solely as perennials were once consid-

ered herbs. Some herbs, like yarrow and monarda, provide a long season of color; silvery herbs such as

artemisia and lamb's ears add variety and harmony to the garden; a big stand of bronze fennel or a free-

flowering shrub rose adds bulk as well as texture and color; tall herbs such as angelica and monkshood are handsome in the back of the border, while others such as catnip and lady's mantle enhance the edges; and all are less troublesome to care for than many more delicate flowers. And if you have a shady garden, various mints, lemon balm, sweet cicely, lamb's ears, chervil, and parsley will happily grow there.

In fact, no matter what your garden needs, there is undoubtedly an herb that can be used to fill them.

As ground covers they are unsurpassed. Chamomile quickly blankets bare areas even in partial shade. Sweet woodruff with its whorls of leaves and tiny white flowers will spread in shady areas under trees where grass finds it tough sledding. Violets, another shade lover, can't be contained if they find the conditions agreeable, and will wander through woodlands or even the grass if you allow it. In sunny spots, woolly yarrow with its silvery foliage and bright yellow flowers or a variety of creeping thymes are attractive and hardy.

In Provence, Jean Mus uses thyme as a ground cover on a terraced garden.

Herbs can also be trained into splendid hedges. In warm climates, both bay and rosemary will grow into thick rows reaching six feet or more in height. Boxwood is the standard for precisely clipped low hedges in formal gardens, but germander, hyssop, and santolina can all be grown close together, then clipped neatly to shape. Lavender, too, lends itself to this purpose and a lavender hedge in full bloom is a

Mediterranean herbs such as lamb's ears and santolina thrive in Provence.

spectacular sight, especially in a rose garden. And among the roses, certain rugosas, musks, and polyanthas will grow into a beautiful but impenetrable flowering barrier. Herbs also work extremely well as edging plants. Imagine how beautiful lady's mantle, catmint, lavender, lamb's ears, silver mound artemisia, or low-growing roses would be spilling out of a border or over a path or surrounding a birdbath.

Perhaps one of the most appealing reasons to garden with herbs is their ease of care. Many are drought-tolerant; most resist diseases and are unattractive to garden pests. Annuals such as basil, borage, coriander, and dill are easily grown from seed, as are certain perennials such as monarda, chives, and fennel. However, slow-growing perennials like thyme and rosemary are best purchased from a nursery or grown from cuttings. Although this book is not intended as a horticultural handbook, you will find basic growing information for the most popular herbs in the chart on page 254.

Because there are so many fresh possibilities for using herbs in the garden, we wanted to bring them together for you in a book. To find the most enticing examples, we have spent the past few years traveling all across the United States and through England and France. From a brilliantly colorful natural garden in the U.S. Northwest to the most disciplined clipped topiary garden in France's

introduction

Provence, herbs have played a major part in the beauty of the gardens we have visited. Over and over again, gardeners suggested we tell our readers that one of the best possible ways to learn about how plants grow and to get ideas for their own gardens is to visit other gardens. We hope that in reading this book you will feel that you have seen these gardens with us. It is filled with large photographs that will give you an overall sense of the garden as well as ideas on how to combine plants and colors effectively. And we've added special sections on all the important aspects of gardening with herbs.

However, a garden is more than plants, so you'll find information on gar-

Two antique stone posts mark a path at Lower Severalls in England.

den seating, walls and fences, garden structures, and more in these pages.

Decorations also add visual interest to a garden and stamp it with the owner's per-

sonality. An old stone trough, a collection of stones, a folk artist's birdhouse, a stone cat perched on a chair, and an old fence post are examples of additions that give these gardens style and will inspire you.

All the gardeners we visited derived enormous pleasure from their gardens. Often they start the day with a cup of coffee in a favorite corner of the garden, watching the bees work busily among the herb blossoms. Many retreat to a favorite spot at the end of a busy day to relax surrounded by sweet scents.

Most even enjoy weeding among the fragrant leaves and flowers. We hope that reading this book will encourage you to join them and learn firsthand the many joys of gardening with herbs.

exuberant
COLOR

When you first see the beautiful

garden surrounding the lovely

sixteenth-century stone Fitz House in

Wiltshire, England, you're immediately

struck by its exuberant colors and lush

plantings. The garden is the joint effort

of Major Mordaunt-Hare and his wife:

the major does most of the gardening

but credits his artistic wife's extraordi-

nary sense of color for the magnificent

result. The Mordaunt-Hares first began gardening in Kent just after they married in 1948. Frequent visits to Sissinghurst, where famous writer Vita Sackville-West herself showed them through her gardens, ignited a lifelong love of gardening that has reached full flower at Fitz House, the home they've occupied for more than forty years.

PRECEDING PAGES: LEFT, Pale roses and white flowers relieve the intense color of blue delphiniums and red valerian (*Centranthus*) in this border. **RIGHT:** A honeysuckle vine drapes the door to one of the outbuildings while lady's mantle grows robustly among the aged stones of the walk. **THIS PAGE:** Masses of lavender and lady's mantle overflow onto the stone path that leads through two carefully clipped yews to the front door, **OPPOSITE.** Partway up the hill, **RIGHT,** roses climb over the thatched summer house. A bench beneath the back lawn's retaining wall beckons visitors to sit surrounded by campanula, lady's mantle, and geraniums, **BELOW.**

The original garden around the house was laid out in the 1920s and extended up the hill to the round summer house. Hedges of clipped yew and beech gave it a semiformal structure that included a charming rose garden; a stone retaining wall made room for a small terrace and a

OVERLEAF: From almost anywhere in the upper garden there is a splendid view of the house and lawn. Here the brilliant chartreuse of lady's mantle and the strong yellow of santolina are tempered by delicate gray foliage.

ABOVE: At Chipping Croft in Gloucestershire, Dr. Taylor has mixed foxglove, delphiniums, mullein, and purple-flowered sage for a glorious display of color. LEFT: In the traditional herb garden at Fort Vancouver in Washington, once the home of the Hudson Bay Trading Company, generous plantings of single varieties of herbs and flowers create a pleasing tapestry of color. BELOW: This border at Jenkyn Place in Hampshire, England, is a simple combination of lavender and yellow roses.

HERBAL COLOR

Herbs are often dismissed as a source of color in the garden, but anyone who has seen the sharp chartreuse of lady's mantle, the deep blue of monkshood, the rich purple of sage and lavender, the soft pink of soapwort, the brilliant yellow of yarrow, or the shaggy red blossoms of monarda knows that these plants have much to offer beyond their fragrance, flavor, and foliage. The soft silvery gray of artemisias, lamb's ears, and others are also an integral part of color planning, adding a sense of harmony to complex color mixtures, highlighting dark corners, or serving as a foil for more brilliant hues.

ABOVE: In one section of the border at Jenkyn Place, the various shapes and yellows of herbs such as verbascum and evening primrose are accented with small touches of pink poppies and orange lilies. Bright pink coneflowers make a colorful display in Sally Whimm's Ohio garden, RIGHT. Golden sage blends with pink roses, BELOW.

ABOVE: A circle of purple lavender frames an old tree trunk that's used as a sundial base at Fort Vancouver. In the background, pale yellow sisyrinchium is underplanted with pansies while rose campion, cornflowers, foxglove, and poppies create a harmonious medley of reds and blues. A dark green jug contrasts handsomely with the sharp chartreuse blooms of lady's mantle in Carol Kelly's Oregon garden, BELOW.

15

Jane Rivkin plants clematis along with roses on this rose pillar, LEFT, to increase color and extend the blooming period. One of the simplest ways to add color and height to a garden is to use simple twig or bamboo supports for flowering climbers like nasturtiums, roses, or morning glories, BELOW.

ABOVE: The bright blue of campanula seems even more intense when seen against the chartreuse flowers of lady's mantle as in this border at Charlton Park in Wiltshire, England. In the herb garden at Fort Vancouver, the brilliant white flowers and silvery foliage of white campion are a lovely foil for the pinks and blues of foxglove, roses, and cornflowers, BELOW.

BELOW: The blues and pinks of perennial geraniums, rose campion, and pinks blend congenially in Carol Kelly's garden, then contrast boldly but not unpleasantly with the vibrant yellow-green of lady's mantle.

The visual impact of color is what you see first in a garden. Placed with a sure hand, color makes an average planting more interesting; approached indifferently, it offends the eye even in the most beautifully laid out garden.

As with most aspects of gardening, there are times when it's more interesting to break the rules, and since color is very personal, there are times when the most unlikely combination can seem right. But until you develop a reliable color sense, it's best to follow a few simple guidelines. Start by limiting yourself to a simple color scheme: choose either warm or cool colors, then add an unexpected accent to bring your garden to life. For example, you might start with a range of blues, purples, and purply pinks, then use a touch of yellow or orange for a visual surprise. Or combine yellows, oranges, and reds and drop in a flash of bright purple for spice.

These limited palettes are really less confining than you might imagine, because each color also has its own warm and cool side—red purples and blue purples, for example—as well as many gradations from pale to dark. Keeping color under

At Camp Cottage in Gloucestershire, England, **ABOVE**, the fifteenth-century thatched cottage is surrounded by an amazing array of plants, all grown from seed or cuttings. Their varying bloom times assure an ongoing display of color. Yellow foliage from conifers as well as such herbs as lady's mantle and golden marjoram can be as effective as flowers in coloring a border, as evidenced at Brook Lodge Farm in Surrey, England, **RIGHT**.

ABOVE: Early in the English summer, roses, lady's mantle, lavender, and campanula fill the border at Cerney House with color. When they are in bloom, poppies add a bright accent.

ABOVE: Patches of white feverfew highlight the path leading through the roses to the sixteenth-century thatched farmhouse at Bundels in Devon, England, helping the visitor to find his way, even by moonlight. The overall color feeling in the herb garden at Fort Vancouver, RIGHT, is based on variations of red, white, and blue, but touches of yellow and orange keep it from being boring.

control this way is especially important in a small garden where the eye takes in everything at once.

When planting a long border, or several different areas in the garden, you can introduce more colors, but avoid harsh juxtapositions. Let the palest tones of one group gradually meld into the paler tones of the next, or add white flowers or gray foliage to ease the transition. You could also let the colors flow as they would around a color wheel, blue blending

into purple, then pink, and finally red, orange, and yellow. Either method provides a harmonious effect.

Try to have each color flowing into the next, best achieved by planting at least three or more of one variety together. Single plantings are spotty and deliver no color message, especially when seen from a distance. Use the contrast of pales and darks to avoid visual boredom.

Bright sun tends to wash out colors, so follow nature's example and use strong colors in hot, sunny climates. Paler colors and white will show to greater advantage in shady areas. White, of course, lightens up any color palette and can often be as brilliant as a strong color. And when you're planting, don't overlook the many shades of green, from palest lime to silvery gray. They continue to add interest and diversity to the garden long after all the blossoms are gone.

For a short time in the spring, the magenta flowers of chives and thyme add extra color to the path lined with long-blooming catmint and lady's mantle in my garden, ABOVE. This spectacular display of color in the Park and Tilford garden in Vancouver, TOP RIGHT, is achieved through a simple combination of catnip and Prima Ballerina, Gene Boerner, and Redgold roses. In Elaine Kheene's garden near Seattle, silvery artemisia, golden marjoram, and wispy grasses add as much color and texture as the flowers, RIGHT.

THE pleasures OF PROVENCE

Anne Cox Chambers has created a microcosm of Provence at her charming home near Saint-Rémy, France. Vineyards line the drive, bees hum happily in the field of lavender below the terrace, and in the distance, a grove of olive trees covers the hillside.

When Mrs. Chambers bought Le Petit Fontanille, an old Provençal *mas* (farm),

PRECEDING PAGES: Wooden fencing on low stone walls and graceful gates define the two sections of the Colonial garden, LEFT. In the potager, RIGHT, carefully trimmed box hedge echoes the spherical shape of the topiary.

there was little more around the house than a few nice old trees, a stairway leading up the hill to no particular destination, and an allée of cypress trees. What might have been a lawn was bare earth, and a barnyard lay where there is now a terrace. She called upon the late Peter Coates, a respected English garden designer, to help her plan the bones of the garden, a project he undertook with great sensitivity to the site and the local growing conditions, concentrating on native vegetation like micocoulier trees, santolina, cypress, and other Mediterranean plants. "The soil here is very limey," explains Mrs. Chambers, "so we can't grow any azaleas or rhododendrons," both of which thrive in her native Georgia. "The plants that do best here are those that like lime and that the rabbits don't like." Fortunately there is water on the property (Fontanille means source), so it was possible to add a lawn, though not enough to maintain a typical English garden.

The field of lavender below the house was already in place. "Peter thought it had probably originally been grown as a market crop, not a garden," she says, "so we left it that way." In order to make the existing olive orchard visible from the house, they removed trees and bushes that were blocking the view. The olives are harvested in November and some of the crop is kept for eating, while the remainder goes to the local mill in Massaune to be pressed for olive oil.

The space between the olive grove and the lavender field was transformed into a colonial-style garden with two main sections. On one side, herbs, vegetables, and flowers are arranged in the colorful patterns typical of a potager, or

Facing the house across the lawn, a formal rose garden is enclosed within neatly clipped box hedges, RIGHT, each section punctuated by an olive tree pruned into an enormous sphere.

PRECEDING PAGES: An army of boxwood balls marches across the lawn beneath a hillside planted with masses of lavender, santolina, Russian sage, and other plants that grow freely, providing a pleasant contrast to the controlled garden below. THIS PAGE: RIGHT, A bench is almost hidden by artemisia. A lush bay laurel hedge separates the potager from the lavender field, where the sweet smell of lavender joins the pungent scent of the tall rosemary hedge edging the center pathway, BELOW.

Mrs. Chambers collects old stone statuary, BELOW, on forays to local antiques dealers and places them enticingly throughout the garden. The Colonial garden, OPPOSITE, was situated to receive full sun. Box hedges define the simple plan of the potager, planned with the help of noted English gardener Rosemary Verey. The bold leaves of chard and ornamental cabbage provide a textural contrast for clay tile edging and smooth stone balls.

kitchen garden, while on the other side country flowers grow in gay abandon among the herbs.

The garden is an ongoing project, and most recently Mrs. Chambers has transformed what was once a tennis court into a precisely patterned garden surrounded by armies of spherical boxwood. The final section of this garden is an aromatic border. "Every plant here is either sweet-smelling or edible," she says. At the end is a hedge, behind which hides a "secret garden" that visitors are urged to explore. A modern version of the old Italian water gardens where pathside fountains are activated by the footsteps of visitors, it comes as an especially welcome treat here in the hot Provençal countryside.

TRADITIONAL GARDENS

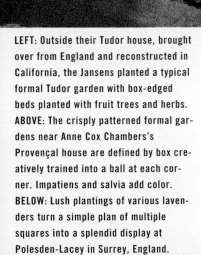

LEFT: Outside their Tudor house, brought over from England and reconstructed in California, the Jansens planted a typical formal Tudor garden with box-edged beds planted with fruit trees and herbs.
ABOVE: The crisply patterned formal gardens near Anne Cox Chambers's Provençal house are defined by box creatively trained into a ball at each corner. Impatiens and salvia add color.
BELOW: Lush plantings of various lavenders turn a simple plan of multiple squares into a splendid display at Polesden-Lacey in Surrey, England.

To the uninitiated, the possibilities of an herb garden begin and end with the traditional symmetrically segmented descendants of monastic kitchen gardens. Yet there are many possible variations on this basic layout, ranging from simple to elaborate, and all of them are appealing. The structure of these gardens is based on two central paths that intersect in the center at right angles, precisely dividing the area into squares and rectangles. A traditional garden is often enclosed with a wall, a fence, or a hedge with one or more entrances through an arbor or a gate. The resulting space is balanced and calm.

To create a traditional garden, find a sunny spot, decide upon the size, then draw the plan on graph paper. Next, clear the site, prepare the soil, and carefully transfer the design from paper to the ground, measuring accurately and using stakes and string to mark the outlines. Prepare the paths, which can be anything from brick to wood chips, depending upon the degree of formality you are seeking. Define the planting areas with some type of edging.

The garden can be devoted to culinary herbs, fragrant herbs, medicinal herbs, or any mixture that pleases you. If you want more color than you think herbs will provide, add a few flowers. For a very formal garden, outline each section in

TOP LEFT: Jodie Slaymaker used barberry and germander to make a simple knot pattern In her Nashville garden. Frequently the intersection of paths is marked with a fountain or a sundial as in Nancy Riley's traditional herb garden in Maine, ABOVE. LEFT: When Carole Saville moved from New Jersey to California she took her herbs with her and created a traditional herb garden reminiscent of the one she had left behind. Enclosing the garden with a hedge and clipping a large rosemary into a spherical shape gave this area a certain formality in the otherwise informal garden.

a trim herbal hedge of germander or box and plant precisely, allowing enough room between plants so that each can be seen distinctly. For a more informal effect, place the plants so close they seem to grow together and spill out into the paths. While the charming result of this type of planting has an air of naturalness, the basic design will maintain some degree of order.

Knot gardens, extremely popular in the seventeenth century, are another traditional form. These are intricate patterns of trim little herbal hedges that appear to cross over and under each other, but in reality the effect comes from a contrast in the color of the foliage and meticulous trimming. The designs can be very complicated or as simple as two interlocking circles easy enough to be attempted by any gardener.

LEFT: Elaine Burden created a small formal area in a secluded corner of her garden by enclosing a sundial and a geometric planting with a germander hedge. **RIGHT:** Using bricks to define the area, Pat Beckman set a traditional raised-bed herb garden in the lawn.

RIGHT: In Normandy, Mark Brown's herb garden, the long narrow shape of which echoes that of the French farmhouse it faces, is composed of a double row of square beds.

LEFT: Although Joanne Shea's Virginia garden stands in the middle of the lawn, it is clearly defined by stone edgings and balls of box at the corners. The dovecote creates a focal point. The paths are wide enough to accommodate a mower. BELOW: Linda Veffer used brick paths with brick edgings to emphasize the diamond shape of the herb garden just outside her kitchen door. A picket fence separates it from the surrounding open spaces.

The most important requirement is patience, as it will take at least two seasons for small plants to become a hedge.

Patterns can be adapted from plans in old garden books or even from a design in a rug or Moorish tile. Draw the plan on graph paper first, then transfer it to the garden. Select plants whose colors will help delineate the pattern and place them close enough together so they grow into a hedge. Some of the most popular herbs for knot gardens are germander, box-wood, lavender, hyssop, santolina, thyme, and barberry.

LEFT: The herb garden within the walls of Holland's Frans Hals Museum, laid out on a variation of the traditional four-square plan, is defined with brick edgings. Local shells are used in place of gravel in the paths.

AN OHIO yankee

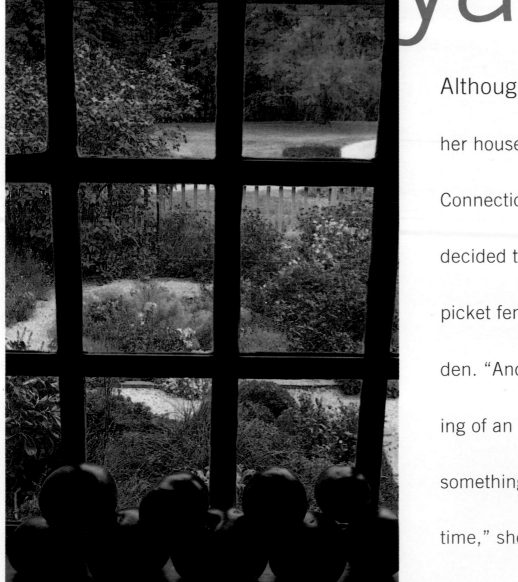

Although Elaine Shea lives in Ohio, her house reminds her of an old Connecticut farmhouse, so when she decided to add a garden, she wanted a picket fence and a traditional herb garden. "And I wanted it to have the feeling of an English cottage garden, with something popping into bloom all the time," she says.

PRECEDING PAGES: The fragrant mounds of mint and lemon balm planted near the bench, LEFT, enhance both the pleasure of a relaxing moment in the garden and Elaine's cuisine. Her kitchen window, RIGHT, overlooks the herb garden, inspiring her as she plans menus. OPPOSITE: Siting the Colonial kitchen garden in the ell made by the kitchen wing and the house, provides both a sense of structure and protection from strong winds.

Since Elaine likes to cook, she situated the garden outside the kitchen door for convenience. For the design, she looked through old gardening books for inspiration, but relied on her own eye to determine the final shape, deviating from the expected rectangle in order to utilize every available inch of space next to the drive. Once the simple garden design was laid out, the beds were edged with brick, which also defines a small sitting area against the house.

Planting has been an ongoing project, with the garden evolving over the years. Originally the sundial was surrounded by thyme, but "I wanted more color," says Elaine, "so I planted anemones instead." Now the anemones have grown so big she is planning to move them and replace them with a low-growing plant that will provide a greater contrast in height. There have been other changes, too. "If a plant doesn't grow well in the garden, it's out. Sometimes I decide I don't like those that do do well, and they're out, too," she admits.

Replacements may be divisions or cuttings from friends, or a plant that Elaine has researched on winter days when it's too cold to garden. But even on such days reminders of the garden are close at hand, as she sips a cup of herb tea brewed from a blend of the orange mint, spearmint, and peppermint that she dried during the summer.

Gravel paths and the slightly asymmetrical design keep the garden, TOP, from becoming too formal. Herbs and flowers spill lavishly out over the gravel walks, adding to the garden's informality, LEFT. Bush basil, a good edging, tumbles over a walk, RIGHT.

Sag Harbor, on the eastern end of Long Island, is filled with handsome historic houses dating from its days as a busy whaling center. Among them is a late Greek Revival house built by a wealthy merchant in the 1860s that is now owned by Joy and Bob Lewis. The Lewises were attracted to the house as much by its

A DESIGNER'S garden

large south-facing garden as by the architecture, and in fact started work on the garden even before they began the remodeling they had planned.

Bob, an interior designer and avid gardener, is a native Virginian, and as he glances around the garden now he finds the brick walks and the trees and shrubs he planted, such as boxwood, magnolia, holly, and a Ben Franklin tree, lend a Southern feeling. But ideas came from other sources as well: the long walk that forms the axis

of the garden was inspired by one at the Van Cortlandt manor house on the Hudson River, while the plan of the kitchen garden was based on a photograph of a charming French potager he once saw in a magazine.

Neatly clipped yew hedges divide the garden into three "rooms," each one planted to relate to the rooms from which it is visible. From the front of the house forward, roses, most

PRECEDING PAGES, LEFT: The house is painted Bob's signature putty, a color derived from the leaves of an American beech in winter that is a perfect foil for colorful herbs and flowers. In the rose garden, Mary Rose, a favorite, flowers generously. The roses are underplanted with herbs such as santolina, dianthus, lavender, thyme, and Johnny-jump-ups. RIGHT: A bust from a local antiques store calmly surveys the garden surrounded by plume poppy, mullein, campanula, and crambe. THIS PAGE, LEFT AND ABOVE: Foxgloves are allowed to reseed freely, adding striking vertical accents all through the garden. In late spring they are complemented by iris, poppies, and catmint. The protection of a south-facing wall and heat-retaining bricks, OPPOSITE, creates a microclimate more hospitable to tender plants and encourages early blooming.

from British rosarian David Austin, blossom throughout the summer, to be admired from the sitting room. "I use a drip system to water the roses to avoid black spot," says Bob, "and since the soil here was full of clay, I rototilled topsoil and peat into it before we laid out the garden, to improve the drainage."

Beyond the first yew hedge lies the double parterre, which provides a

LEFT AND BELOW: Flowers, herbs, and vegetables mix happily in the kitchen garden, which is separated from the parterre by a beautifully shaped yew hedge. Flowering sage, chives, nasturtium, and lavender add brilliant color to the greens of such plants as lettuce and parsley. In general, each bed is devoted to a single variety with the occasional intrusion of a self-seeded foxglove. Other volunteers spring up in the gravel paths. When winter snows fall, the precise geometric structure of the potager still provides a sense of the garden and a pleasing view from the kitchen window. The kitchen terrace, RIGHT, is another of Bob's microclimates. Facing south and warmed by the sun, it is protected from winds on two sides by the walls of the house. Potted double box balls and a potted grandiflora magnolia thrive in this benign atmosphere.

OPPOSITE: The colorful parterre is filled with cosmos, foxglove, and nicotiana that have self-seeded. The Gothic folly in the background, designed by Bob, will be part of the next section of the garden. RIGHT, BELOW LEFT AND RIGHT: Blue, pink, and white flowers predominate in the colorful parterre. Herbs are secondary in this part of the garden, but sage, poppies, and foxglove add herbal color and those with gray foliage, like lamb's ears, are mixed in for balance. Many of the plants were selected to encourage butterflies and birds. Two large box balls accent the diamond pattern.

pleasing vista from the library and dining room. "This spot was windier than we expected," explains Bob, "but once the hedges are established, they'll give the needed protection." The strictly formal plan has been planted informally, but acts as a check to keep the lush growth within bounds and to give structure to the garden even in winter.

Outside the kitchen door is the third garden room, a potager, based on a simple plan of square raised beds surrounded by gravel paths. Here herbs and vegetables are the stars. "Everything we've grown here has been very successful,"

says Bob. "The beds are raised just enough for great drainage and the height makes them easy to harvest. In addition, the gravel in the walks warms up early, making it possible for me to plant lettuces earlier in the season. The chives come up early, too. I like the idea of pushing a microclimate," he adds.

"I like the sense of continuity that this garden represents," says Joy. "Even though the original garden in France that inspired it no longer exists, this one carries on the idea. I think this frequently happens in gardening. It's like passing a tradition down through the family."

43

KITCHEN GARDENS/ edible flowers

No cook should be without an herb garden, preferably planted close to the kitchen door. When space is limited, it might be nothing more than a window box garden or large barrel planted with the herbs used most (or those that are most difficult to find at the market). But if space permits, plan a proper garden that will accommodate herbs for daily use and some to dry for winter stews or fragrant bouquets.

ABOVE: The informal nature and decorations of Joan Lathy's kitchen garden are very sympathetic to the rustic log cabin. RIGHT: The intricately shaped box-edged sections of the kitchen garden at Bourton House in Gloucestershire are separated by stone pavers and planted with a wide selection of herbs, vegetables, and berries. TOP RIGHT: Terracotta forcers are handsome garden ornaments when not in use.

ABOVE: The modern look of tiers of raised beds complements a contemporary California house and also serves the practical purpose of separating various crops and providing more planting space. BELOW: A splendid scarecrow stands watch over one of the box-edged sections of the Tudor-style kitchen garden at Littlecote House in Berkshire, England. Based on the traditional four-square plan, the sections are planted with herbs and vegetables. Here, santolina and lavender surround a bamboo support for beans and separate various crops.

At Sooke Harbour House on Vancouver Island, LEFT AND BELOW, the vast gardens surrounding the inn contain over 550 types of herbs, vegetables, and edible flowers, all of which find their way into the innovative dishes for which the kitchen is known. BOTTOM RIGHT: Herbs are planted in neat rows in the kitchen garden outside Mary and Joe Flegle's original 1790 log cabin.

For twelve hundred years, the traditional kitchen garden has been based on a four-square plan like those in the old monastery gardens. The most elaborate versions, inspired by the beautiful potager designed for Louis XIV at Versailles, are a lovely mix of herbs, vegetables, and flowers, the carefully plotted beds organized in colorful geometric patternings that are charming but labor-intensive to keep looking their best.

A less ambitious gardener might plant a tiny potager or design a checkerboard pattern that alternates growing spaces with square stones; cultivate a small garden between the rungs of an old orchard ladder or the spokes of an old carriage wheel; or simply tuck culinary herbs into the landscape all through the garden.

Any kitchen garden is prettier with the addition of edible

LEFT: Ryan Gainey's potager is contained within the brick foundation of an old greenhouse. The plan is based on three diamonds laid end to end. Such herbs as thyme, nasturtiums, and box are used as edgings around chard, poppies, onions, and other herbs and vegetables. The center of each diamond is marked with a Fairy rose standard. TOP: Karen Cauble's country kitchen garden is based on a triangular plan defined by simple log edgings. More logs, propped on supports of crossed tree limbs, are used to make a fence with the same country feeling. ABOVE: In another section of the kitchen garden at Littlecote, lavender shares space with rhubarb growing in a terra-cotta forcer, bamboo-staked tomatoes, artichokes, and other herbs and vegetables.

BOTTOM: Denise Adams mixes flowers with herbs in her Ohio kitchen garden, then defines the space with a white picket fence. RIGHT AND BELOW: The Berganzers' lush Georgia garden, located just outside the kitchen door, combines flowers and decorative herbs such as lamb's ears with culinary favorites. Stone paths divide the raised beds, which are companionably edged in local stone.

flowers. They're colorful and sometimes tasty, too, and even when they have little or no flavor, they make lovely garnishes for everything from soup to dessert. The blossoms of all culinary herbs, from the pretty little blooms of thyme and scented geraniums to the more spectacular flowers of sage and monarda, are edible. So are pansies, hollyhocks, begonias, primroses, roses, lemon gem marigolds, calendula, and lilies, among others.

A few words of caution, however. Any flower you plan to eat must be grown organically and in a place where it is protected from automobile exhausts and other pollutants. And since many flowers are poisonous, among them monkshood and foxglove, don't eat any flower unless you are certain it is safe.

In June, the spectacular border outside the walled garden at Cerney House is in full bloom, mounds of sharp chartreuse lady's mantle contrasting dramatically with the tall, graceful spires of foxglove that punctuate the planting. It is a fitting intro-duction to the delightful garden that stretches

A GLORIOUS ENGLISH border

On the edges of a charming Cotswold village, Dr. and Mrs. Peter Taylor have created a lush Eden. Like many town gardens throughout England, this one is invisible from the street, hidden behind an unremarkable stone wall. The small gate next to the house gives no hint of the glorious two-acre garden that lies beyond.

An ENGLISH treasure

When the Taylors moved here from London, the garden contained little more than some good trees and a morass of thistles. Great patience and prodigious work has transformed it into a magnificent display of herbs and flowers. Trees and shade-loving plants border a lovely lawn ending near the house at the bottom of a steep terraced slope that supports several distinct gardens.

The lower garden, resting on a handsome stone wall, leads away from the house along a wide gravel path that runs the entire length of the garden. "There was nothing here but the

path when we arrived," says Dr. Taylor. "We brought the box from our London garden." Now the path is bordered on both sides by a glorious combination of catmint, lady's mantle, sage, and box, while overhead roses and clematis tumble over a series of arbors. The path leads to a bench from which to enjoy the garden and listen to the happy serenades of birds.

A short flight of stairs leads to the next level, where an old shed-turned-garden house boasts a tiny terrace overlooking the gardens. The large formal garden adjacent to it is based on a circle, a square, and an oval, but planted so exuberantly that the precise patterning is almost hidden.

On the third and final level, the Taylors grow most of the

PRECEDING PAGES: A gently curved path in the lower garden leads to a bench on which to enjoy the spectacular display of color put on by lady's mantle, catmint, delphinium, and roses, LEFT. The simple entry, RIGHT, belies the glorious garden that lies beyond. THIS PAGE: Alliums, fennel, and the bright orange edible flowers of calendula, LEFT, are among the varied plantings in the formally laid-out herb garden. Roses and some of the thirty varieties of clematis grown in the garden climb the arbors along the path, ABOVE. Golden foliage accents the feeling of color provided by the herbs and flowers, OPPOSITE.

vegetables for their table. Since they also grow their own mushrooms, they have a steady source of mushroom compost to feed the garden. Fish blood and bonemeal are also added to the soil, especially in the spring, because of their long-lasting benefits.

Although his only previous gardening experience was

growing vegetables during World War II, Dr. Taylor has become a devoted gardener, spending most of his time now that he is retired either planning or planting. "I plan something out in my head first," he says, "then put it on paper." Once in place, the plan is often adjusted. "Some things disappoint you; they're not what you want," he adds. "When that happens, I just put them elsewhere. Color combinations, for example, are a very personal thing. Sometimes colors that clash are more fun. The important thing is that the garden grows as a cohesive unit."

Although the Cotswold climate is kind to gardeners, the temperature has been known to drop below freezing, though never for very long. "And we tend to have latish frosts when the trees are already in bloom," he says. "That's bad for the plums and good for the pears. But you make do with nature," he adds. "You can't go against it, that's for sure."

PRECEDING PAGES: Above a retaining wall, Dr. Taylor's lower garden is a kaleidoscope of colors and shapes. Poppies and spires of foxglove and delphinium thrust skyward. The old stone wall and restored garden house are in the background. BELOW: An old stone urn is framed by lamb's ears, thyme, and santolina. Box outlines the exuberantly planted geometric beds in the herb garden, OPPOSITE. Mullein and foxgloves are encouraged to grow where they self-seed and golden sage adds color to the garden even without flowers. The varied shades of green foliage are as important to the garden's palette as are the flowers themselves.

LEFT: A harmonious color scheme, mass plantings, and a repeating planting pattern make this curvy border in Jane Rivkin's Long Island garden extremely pleasing. BELOW: Climbing roses provide a nice background for the colorful border at Manor Farm in Wiltshire, England. Mounds of lady's mantle, pinks, and other low growers contrast interestingly with more linear plants. The spectacular double border at Jenkyn Place in Hampshire, England, OPPOSITE, is a splendid example of how breaking the rules and bringing some tall plants forward makes a more interesting display.

BORDERS

Thoughts of an English garden bring visions of exuberant borders filled with masses of colorful plants. There are often herbs scattered throughout these borders, contributing color, interesting foliage, and heady fragrance. This happy mixture is an inheritance from the Middle Ages, when little distinction was made between herbs and flowers, since almost every plant in the garden served a useful purpose and was therefore considered herbal.

By definition, borders are beds that have a background—a building, a wall, a hedge, or a fence. They might be a narrow strip, but they are truly at their best when they are a generous 7 to 8 feet deep, allowing for a lush layering of plants.

When a border is more than 6 feet wide, a narrow strip at the back of the bed allows access to the plants without crushing them. Occasional stepping-stones serve the same purpose, but may leave an unsightly bare spot.

Lamb's ears, lady's mantle, catnip, lemon balm, and lavender are just a few of the perennial herbs that can be used to good effect at the front of the border. Farther back, peonies, poppies, monarda, bronze fennel, monkshood, mullein, artemisias, yarrow, and roses perform reliably year after year.

Since contemporary borders are planted primarily with labor-saving perennials, the soil should be well prepared before being planted, as this will be the last chance to really work it over without disturbing roots. Dig to a depth of at least 1 foot; 2 feet would be better. Add fertilizer, organic humus to make the soil friable, and, if it is heavy, some builder's sand to improve drainage. Check the pH and add lime if necessary.

There are a few guides to planting a successful border. To keep it looking good all season long, you should consider blooming time and color. One of the easiest ways to ensure continuous bloom and color is using a planting plan with an acetate overlay for each month of the growing season. Color in the plants that will bloom each month and you will quickly see how the color is distributed. (For more information on how to use color, see page 14.) In organizing your border, plan to place at least three of each variety together in a triangular formation, leaving enough room around each plant for it to grow to full size. Most perennials will need to be divided after 2 to 3 years, giving you more plants for another part of the garden or for friends. Repeat planting groups periodically along the length of the border to give a sense of unity and rhythm.

ABOVE: Roses frame a border at Little Bowden in Berkshire, England, while occasional stalks of deep blue delphinium add visual interest to the rest of the border's low-growth plan. In Los Angeles, Dominique Dominguez-Branne has combined pink, lavender, and white with gray foliage in a cool border more reminiscent of England than California, ABOVE RIGHT. RIGHT: The drive at Chisenbury Priory in Wiltshire, England, is bordered with a glorious display of color from such plants as catmint, delphinium, lady's mantle, and euphorbia. The spiny gray foliage of thistle is an unexpected accent.

Plant height is another important factor in creating attractive borders. The general rule is tall plants at the back of the border, medium-tall plants in the center, and low, sprawling plants at the front. Like all rules, however, this one is best broken judiciously, to give the border more interest. You'll find a spire of foxglove, for example, may look just right near the front of the border, where it has self-sown.

Be aware of shapes and texture. Juxtaposing a low, rounded plant like Silver Mound artemisia or catnip with spires of foxglove or mullein adds interest, as does the contrast of furry lamb's ears with spiky lavender. In wide borders, consider adding shrubs and small flowering trees for structure. Interplanting with bulbs and annuals will add ongoing color and camouflage holes left by spent perennials. Above all, be prepared to admit mistakes and rearrange plants until the border is the luxurious display of your dreams.

TOP RIGHT: Although relatively new, the border in Pat Rodgers's Somerset garden is enviably lush. A topiary yew tree is an unexpected but successful addition. **ABOVE:** Ryan Gainey uses herbs, flowers, and small shrubs to give his narrow border interest and structure all through the seasons. **RIGHT:** Herbs and flowers mix companionably in this hillside border at Knightshayes in Devon.

AN ANTIQUES
dealer's
GARDEN

Jackie Butera is an antiques dealer and artist as well as a gardener, but she never had an herb garden until she saw the one across the street from a shop she once had in Skipjack, Pennsylvania. "After I saw that garden, I came home and replaced the vegetables and everything else with herbs," she says. The garden and the projects inspired by the herbs she grows there have become an

PRECEDING PAGES: The kitchen garden, LEFT, enclosed with a picket fence and accessible by slate stepping stones, is decorated with an old pump, straw hats, and a decoy. On the little porch outside the kitchen, RIGHT, old buckets, dried herbs, herb vinegars, and tomatoes are ready to be put to use. THIS PAGE: A blue wheelbarrow and a rustic bird feeder placed just outside the kitchen garden, BELOW, enhance the country feeling. LEFT AND OPPOSITE: The main garden lies behind the house, enclosed by a picket fence with whirligigs perched on three corners, a birdhouse on the fourth. A trip to France inspired the crushed oyster shell path, although similar paths are common in Virginia and Delaware, where shellfishing is an important industry.

extension of her art work, and since her shop is now in an old barn near her house, she has more time to enjoy both. Herbs have even become part of her business: she lectures and offers tours of her garden, and makes potpourris and other herbal items for the shop.

Jackie approaches her gardens visually, arranging the plants for color, size, and texture. The primary herb garden is enclosed by a picket fence, like an outdoor room in the center of the lawn. She sited the garden here to keep the herbs away from the shade trees around the house so they could receive enough sun. A smaller, more informally planted herb garden is located just outside the kitchen door for easy accessibility at mealtimes. Both gardens are decorated with objects that Jackie has collected on antiquing trips. A relaxed gardener, Jackie claims, "I just don't make gardening a big hassle. I have a few old tools, an old cultivator I found here when we moved in, and a garden weasel." She is a

relentless pruner, though she doesn't mulch very much or protect her plants from the Pennsylvania winter, with the exception of a few lavenders that are covered with pine boughs. "I think that's all unnecessary work. It's harder to weed through mulch, and if you go through with a tool instead, you cultivate at the same time and have nice soft ground." Insects are kept under control with "Nana's Bug Juice," a mixture made from six cloves of garlic, a cup of vinegar and 3 cups of water, and some cayenne that is blended, steeped for 3 days, strained, and applied to plants with a spray bottle. Working in the garden every morning keeps weeds in check. "I don't feel like it's a terrible chore," she says. "I love it at seven A.M. when I go out and have coffee. The bees are all out, the aroma is heavenly."

Pat Petrondi comes by her love of flowers naturally: her grandmother and grandfather were florists. Her first garden, planted years ago when her children were young, was created primarily to provide flowers for the dried arrangements Pat wanted in her new house. For greater variety, she supplemented her harvest with weeds

A WREATH MAKER'S garden

carefully chosen from nearby fields. When friends admired a bouquet she'd made, more often than not Pat ended up sending it home with them.

When a local store advertised for someone to do dried flowers, Pat's career as "The Weed Lady" took off. Her hobby has grown into such a thriving enterprise that her husband, Jim, now works full-time farming the herbs and flowers she needs.

"I grow herbs primarily to make wreaths," says Pat, "although I do fool around with a little cooking." When they bought this farmhouse, there was already a garden with some herbs growing. "I figured the farmer who had lived here knew where the sun was best," she says, "so I decided to plant my garden in the same place."

PRECEDING PAGES: The herb garden's raised beds, LEFT, are filled with lamb's ears, lavender, and catnip, all good candidates to dry for use in wreaths and bouquets. RIGHT: The wreath hanging on the side of the barn is one of Pat's special touches. It is made from artemisia, yarrow, globe amaranth, and tansy, and encircles a bee skep. THIS PAGE, OPPOSITE: This garden derives much of its charm from the generous plantings of individual herb varieties. Lamb's ears and sage encircle a small sundial in one section of the garden, TOP. Birdhouses planted just outside the garden, BELOW, focus attention there rather than pulling the eye to another spot.

She started by preparing the ground. With her daughter's help, she dug 3 feet of manure from the abandoned chicken coop into the soil. "I think that's the reason this garden has been so successful," Pat says. Although herb gardeners generally avoid heavy fertilizing, which can lessen the amount of essential oils in the leaves, resulting in less pungent flavors, for Pat's business size takes precedence over taste. "People say herbs don't need good soil," she says, "but I disagree. We dig four to six inches of mushroom compost into the beds every year and people are always amazed at how big my plants are. They grow in leaps and bounds. Even annuals are huge in one month's time."

Raised beds were used to define the individual planting areas, which were then enclosed with simple fencing. Since nine acres of land for field growing extend behind the garden, the fence gives the garden some needed structure. The homemade fencing, in keeping with the country feeling of the property, gave the Petrondis a practical and decorative solution for a relatively small investment.

For laying out the beds, Pat relied on a mental image rather than a planting chart. "I knew I wanted artemisias, sage, thyme, rosemary, lemon verbena, mints—anything that I can dry and use in my wreaths," she recalls. "And there are flowers growing in the garden, too, because I like color."

The old chicken house, ABOVE, is used for storing herbs and flowers, but the outside is always decorated with wreaths, old tools, even a wasp nest, to make a handsome backdrop for the garden. The old washhouse, LEFT, now serves more usefully as a drying shed.

ABOVE LEFT: Mary Emmerling's free-standing Long Island herb garden is set off by a simple picket fence. The cheerful mix of herbs and flowers is enhanced with folk art decorations. ABOVE RIGHT: Dulcey Mahar placed this box-edged garden in the lawn behind her house in Portland, Oregon, so it would be in her line of vision as she worked, then filled it with a combination of herbs and flowers. LEFT: The only entrance to Eve Davis's enclosed Atlanta garden is through a rose-covered arbor. Although primarily a kitchen garden, it also contains flowers and more ornamental herbs such as artemisia and lamb's ears. At Knightshayes in Devon, England, a moss-covered cement ornament stands in a bed of catmint, BELOW.

freestanding beds can be advantageous when the middle of the lawn is the only place that receives enough direct sunlight to ensure healthy plants, or when every conceivable space beside a wall, a fence, or a path has already been planted and the gardener simply can't stop gardening. However, it's important that the bed relate to the rest of the garden, or at least to that part of it that the eye takes in at the same time.

The island should have the same overall feeling as the main garden: a geometric space if the garden is a formal one; free-form for a less structured ambience. Use the same kind of edging that appears elsewhere, and try to place the bed so that it relates spatially in some way to an existing garden or building. Although it may compromise the isolation of a freestanding planting, a path can help tie it into the rest of the garden.

In planting an island bed, however, the tallest plants should always go in the center, with heights diminishing as you work toward the outer edges. It is especially important to remember that the bed will be seen from all sides.

If it is a large bed, you may want to place a few stepping-stones in the garden to facilitate weeding and general care.

Bunny Van Valey's New Hampshire garden is a series of freestanding spaces. In the view at RIGHT, the plants grow around the edges of a sunken patio. Almost all of the plants come from cuttings, foraging, or friends. In another area of Bunny's modular garden, BELOW, a stone retaining wall has been incorporated to compensate for the slope of the land.

THE shapely HERB

Descending the narrow street in the ancient Provençal hill town of Bonnieux, it is difficult to imagine the original and spectacular garden hidden behind the simple walls of Nicole de Vésian's old stone house. Nicole, a former trend forecaster, was already living in an old converted chapel on the other side of this unspoiled French hill town

PRECEDING PAGES: Reflecting the strong shapes elsewhere in the garden, a few of the old trees, LEFT, have been fearlessly cut back to the trunk from the ground up to give them a sculptured shape. An English artist helped Nicole create the handsome sculpture near the entrance from a few carefully selected stones and an ancient hand-hewn watering trough she found in the ruins, RIGHT. THIS PAGE: A layer of small stones carpets the sunny terrace near the lavender field.

when she began to consider retirement several years ago. One day fate led her to an old, tumbledown house that had just become available. She realized the great potential hidden behind the ramshackle ruin and envisioned a terraced garden that would take advantage of the spectacular views across the valley. But it was really the beautiful old stones in the house and garden that drew her to the site and prompted her to make an offer on the house.

Although unable to move into the house for six months, Nicole began work on the garden immediately, clearing away the accumulated debris so she could start planting a garden in its place. Work began with the terrace opening out from the house, then gradually proceeded down the hill. During the restoration, every one of the much-admired stones was carefully saved and reused. Some were

rescued from the house to become steps that connect the upper and lower terraces. And when the wall buttressing part of the terrace collapsed, those stones were used to pave an interior floor.

Nicole relies most heavily on those herbs native to the Mediterranean, such as rosemary, santolina, lavender, sage, and thyme, in this garden, interweaving their textures and colors to provide greater visual interest. "It's like putting objects together. I mix and contrast the volume and the colors of the plants. With even just three different plants you can have so many looks," she notes. Once the plants are in place she adds stone to balance and lighten the overall effect.

Although there are no flowers in the garden, with the exception of a hollyhock (the gift of a bird) and a rose (a

OPPOSITE: Nicole planted a lavender field under the peach trees on the lowest level, then "got bored with it" and ruthlessly deflowered the center section to give the area more visual excitement.

PRECEDING PAGES: The garden is a sweep of sculptured plant material that enchants the eye with its subtle palette of greens, contrasting textures, and carefully disciplined shapes. It was inspired in part by Nicole's memories of a visit to a Chinese garden with spherically shaped plants. THIS PAGE: Large spheres of rosemary and box surround a "found" stone bench, OPPOSITE. Thyme grows defiantly between the stones of the terrace. LEFT AND RIGHT: More examples of the delightful way Nicole incorporates stone in the garden. BELOW: The studio opens onto the upper terrace. From there Nicole can look across the smoothly trimmed green balls to the distant mountains.

present from a friend), it has an irresistible sensual appeal. A few artichokes, grown primarily for their arresting jagged gray leaves, are also allowed to produce their thistlelike blossoms.

Like all extremely personal gardens, this one changes whenever Nicole returns home from the nursery or a friend's garden with a new plant. Sometimes switching or adding one plant starts a chain reaction of moves because the relationship between the colors and sizes has changed.

People find her garden so appealing, requests for her design talents have launched Nicole in a new career designing gardens. She considers the lifestyle of the owner in doing the plan, but the site, the climate, and the type of soil dictate what can be planted. "You have to watch the sun, and consider the heat of summer and the winter, too," she notes. "Every two years we have a few inches of snow and always a few very cold days." And, of course, there is the meager rainfall during the summer months to contend with, as well as the unrelenting winds of the mistral. These demanding weather conditions underscore the practicality of concentrating on herbs and trees native to the region.

But she is most concerned with the relationship between the house and garden. "They must work together," she insists. "After all, life here is lived between the two."

TOPIARY

ABOVE: A charming boxwood basket welcomes visitors to this English house, while two boxwood chairs overlook the garden from the terrace, BELOW.
LEFT: The plump box standards and neatly shaped yew cones in the formal herb garden at Westbury Court in Gloucestershire accent the basic plan and make the garden visually more interesting.

The ancient Romans may well have given birth to that whimsical form of gardening known as topiary, exporting it to France and carrying the tradition with them to England. Today birds and rabbits still parade across lawns along with carefully trimmed spheres, cones, and cubes that give structure and interest to many gardens. Topiary is also an important element of garden architecture: hedges can divide the garden into "rooms" that might even have windows or archways, and trees or shrubs can be trained to make covered walks.

Yews are among the most common shrubs for large in-ground shaping, although some junipers, cypress, and other nonherbal shrubs can be used. Clip an existing shrub back until it is slightly smaller all around than the desired topiary, then cut new growth to the shape you want. Or buy a healthy new plant that is as big as you can afford, but not so big that transplanting will be traumatic. In either case, keep the plant well watered and weeded (mulch will help), and feed the shrub a bit more frequently than you might otherwise. Make sure the shrub has enough room to grow—shaping it does not stop its growth—and for best results, place it in a spot where sun will reach all sides.

Geometric shapes are the easiest to achieve; more complicated shapes require a bit of artistic talent or a preformed wire shape imposed on the bush to guide your shearing. (This

ABOVE: The path leading to a rugged stone bench at Levens Hall in the English Lake District is defined by a hedge and neatly shaped cones of box-wood. At Hascombe Court in Surrey, England, box is trimmed into fanciful shapes to amuse the eye, RIGHT. LEFT: Nicole de Vésian's ruthless pruning gave this ordinary cypress tree a whole new personality.

ABOVE: French fashion designer Bernard Perris raises a pet topiary dove in his Provence garden. Rose topiaries, RIGHT, are produced by grafting and are more delicate than an ordinary rosebush. Protect them in cold winters by loosening the roots, laying the topiary on its side, and covering the roots and stem with a thick layer of soil.

frame disappears beneath the foliage eventually.) Decide upon a shape, then select a healthy shrub with a compatible shape and shear it to an approximate outline. Clip it two or three times per season. Achieving the shape will be a gradual process.

For smaller topiary shapes, the choice of plant material is much greater: santolina, lavender, rosemary, thyme, sage, and box can all be trimmed into round balls like those in Nicole de Vésian's garden, and box, rosemary, and bay will grow tall enough to form cones or even standards. Other herbs, such as lavender, curry plant, scented geraniums, roses, and myrtle, are also good candidates for small standards.

Tiny topiaries are readily available from local or mail-order nurseries, or, with patience, can be grown from a seedling with a single strong stem or a rooted cutting. Place a small bamboo stake in the pot next to the stem and tie it loosely as

LEFT: Another of the fanciful shapes at Hascombe Court. BELOW: Carefully clipped hedges act like living green walls in the garden at Little Bowden in Berkshire, separating the pool area from the rest of the garden while rounded box cones and a rose topiary add interest to a border.

LEFT: An amusing array of boxwood spheres, spirals, and cones line and define a path in the garden at Bourton House in Gloucestershire. A fantasy checker game is always in progress with the topiary chess pieces in the garden at Levens Hall in the English Lake District, ABOVE.

At Het Loo Palace in Holland, **LEFT**, the contrasting shapes and colors of large potted bay standards, cone-shaped yews, and squarely trimmed box heighten the visual interest of the parterre, as do the swirling box arabesques and different colored stone ground cover. Behind the parterre, a masterpiece of topiary forms a green windowed arcade supported by an open-work wooden tunnel, **BELOW LEFT**. Country flowers grow in strictly defined box parterres, **BELOW**, in Anne Cox Chambers's Provençal garden.

it grows, readjusting the ties to make sure they never get too tight. Trim off any side branches, but not the leaves, until the topiary reaches the desired height, then trim off the leaves, pinch out the growing tip, and let it branch. Continue to cut the developing branches until you have a nice full head. This can take anywhere from six months to two years, depending upon the particular plant you are using.

After a long struggle to grow herbs

and flowers in the shade of numerous oak

trees, six years ago I moved to a house set

in the middle of a former potato field with

nary a tree in sight. Setting out to transform

the mud surrounding the house into a

garden, an overwhelming project, I needed

an overall plan to minimize mis-

takes and ensure a cohesive

whole, especially as I was

A WRITER'S garden

PRECEDING PAGES: Several varieties of thyme grow robustly between the pathway's stones, LEFT. The sweet-smelling blossoms of valerian perfume the air during the early summer days, RIGHT. THIS PAGE, LEFT: A privet hedge encloses the rose garden giving the plants protection from the strong winds that sweep across the neighboring fields while providing additional privacy for the entire garden. BELOW: The Robin Hood roses growing along the fence are some of the hardiest roses in the garden. In the spring they are a mass of beautiful red flowers, then bloom intermittently throughout the summer.

planning to do the garden in stages. A consultation with well-known landscape designer Tom Wirth was a serendipitous housewarming present, and together we established the major structural element of the garden: a path running the length of the house with a border on one side and two semicircular beds on the other. It turned the corner and widened into a semicircular patio on the side destined to become a rose garden. Although the garden is based on a square grid, it has a gentler feeling because of the circular patio that reflects the curve of the half-circle beds in front.

Although the garden is uniquely mine, it has been inspired by many of the gardens Chris and I have visited together. The border owes much to a bouquet of purple delphiniums and silvery, purple-flowered lamb's ears with brilliant sprays of chartreuse lady's mantle I saw in an English house. Since I wanted to keep the border totally herbal, I substituted catmint for delphiniums to achieve the same color feeling, and used these three plants repeatedly at the front of the border. Behind them came yarrows of every sort, soapwort, silvery artemisias, rose campion, angelica, valerian, southernwood,

OPPOSITE: In the spring the border is filled with purples and blues, then changes to pinks and purples as the season progresses, always with a touch of yellow to bring out the other colors.

meadow rue and meadow sweet, coneflower, a few roses, and others.

Drawing on memories of the lovely fragrance garden at Alderly Grange, I planted the area facing the rose garden with pinks, heliotrope, valerian, mints, and scented geraniums. These beds are trimly edged in germander, which also hides the cellar window guards. A Fairy rose standard just like those I saw and coveted in Ryan Gainey's garden stands in the center of each.

Creeping thyme gives the bluestone paths the feeling of a long-established garden. The first few plants I tucked in among the stones were almost unnoticeable, but now they require cutting back twice a season.

In other parts of the garden and yard the influences of my fellow gardeners are also apparent. All the wonderful varieties of nicotiana I'd seen in a friend's garden surround my herb shed, and after visiting Major Mordaunt-Hare's garden, I added some centranthus. Robin Hood roses, first seen in Linda Veffer's Ohio garden, grow over the picket fence behind the shed, and near the house, peonies line the white fence behind the crab apple trees, just as they did at my mother's home. Most recently, I've started a small lavender "field," a constant reminder of Provence and the lovely gardens I've visited there.

Like most gardeners, I constantly discover new plants I want to try or an idea I'd like to adapt for my own. But even as I plant new areas and change the existing ones, I will always be reminded of the generous and talented gardeners I've met and their gardens that inspired me.

The semicircular beds are reserved for culinary herbs and edible flowers such as lemon gem marigold, monarda, calendula, nasturtiums, lavender, and Johnny-jump-ups. An assortment of garden ornaments like an old balustrade, an architectural column, and a bench painted the blue of Provence have been collected over the years. Victorian edging tiles from Savannah, Georgia, keep the grass from encroaching on the herbs.

AN ENGLISHWOMAN'S garden

Since the sixteenth century,

Heale House has nestled comfortably in

the Wiltshire countryside. When the

handsome brick and stone house was

requisitioned by the local hospital dur-

ing World War II, the gardens fell into

neglect, but in 1959 Lady Anne Rasch

began the project of restoring them.

PRECEDING PAGES: In the center of the walled tunnel garden, **LEFT**, four box-wood balls from the original garden accentuate the lily pond and provide a focal point for avenues of apple trees. The tunnels are covered with roses, clematis, and honeysuckle. The cottage garden around the converted stable block, **RIGHT**, is a lively mix of roses, thistle, delphinium, and lady's mantle. **THIS PAGE:** Lady Anne softened the large stone terrace by planting lady's mantle, rue, sisyrinchium, and sedum between the stones. The plants on the terrace reseed themselves enthusiastically, necessitating periodic (if somewhat half-hearted) attempts to keep them under control with judicious poisoning.

er husband's great-uncle bought Heale House in 1894, and in 1910 had the noted garden designer Harold Peto plan a formal terrace garden near the house. "They had eight gardeners then," Lady Anne recalls wistfully. When the Rasches arrived at Heale House, however, the herbaceous beds were empty. "Since it was a typical Edwardian planting, there were no shrubs in the border, and all the flowers were gone," says Lady Anne. "At that time we only had one gardener, so we even helped with the mowing." Her original plans for restoring the garden were minimal, but once involved, she gradually undertook more and more.

Since the eight acres are still managed with only two full-time gardeners and some part-time help, her goal was to keep the gardens less labor-intensive. She relied heavily on bulbs and shrubs while eschewing the once-popular bedding out, except for snapdragons that replace the spent tulips in late spring and linger into fall. Low-maintenance shrubs and plants were repeated throughout the garden. "And we planted much too thickly," she says, "because I hate seeing earth." It also helped suppress weeds, another labor-saving move.

The terrace garden designed by Mr. Peto is paved with rugged York stone. Colored foliage borders at the top of the terrace provide year-round interest and a handsome background for roses, peonies, and other perennials. Tall rose-covered pyramids help the borders relate harmoniously to the spacious terrace. A lavender-edged path leads to the house, where similar plantings surround a fishpond.

The walled tunnel garden, which was originally designed as an ornamental rose garden, is one of Lady Anne's favorites. During the war it was used to grow vegetables, but it now contains fruits and flowers as well. "I never thought we'd grow vegetables, but artichokes and asparagus are such little bother and so nice to have," she says. Around the garden, apple and pear espaliers share space with clematis.

Although Lady Anne is modest about her gardening talents, she has created a most appealing garden at Heale House. "There's much too much importance put on permanence," she says. "Changes personalize a garden."

Long-flowering rambler roses from 1920, their names long forgotten, climb over the old stone balustrade, ABOVE. Although the baskets of fruit atop the brick pillars, LEFT, would be at home in the most formal garden, a self-sown mullein growing nearby adds a casual note. RIGHT: Another view of the terrace, where a stray mullein has been allowed to grow undisturbed.

HERBS UNDERFOOT

There are certain herbs that love to be trod upon, giving up their fragrance uncomplainingly and continuing to grow no matter how many steps they endure. These sturdy plants are a boon to those whose gardens are traversed by paths or who have terraces or patios overlooking the garden.

A collection of creeping thymes surrounds an old pump in the garden at the Herb Refuge in Ohio. Letting the plants overflow their borders softens the path, **FAR LEFT.** Mary Emmerling planted herbs and flowers such as alyssum between the stones of her Long Island terrace, **ABOVE.** These plants thrive in only 1- to 2-inch spaces left between the stones, which also protect the roots from extreme heat and cold and eliminate any competition.

Vast expanses of stone uninterrupted by greenery can be cold and intimidating; a plant peeking out here and there lends a more romantic air. Letting plants overflow their borders can soften a path, and tufts of thyme or chamomile, pennyroyal, woolly yarrow, or Corsican mint emerging from cracks along the length of the path is a magnificent sight. It's amazing how little room these plants need to thrive. Leave a 1- to 2-inch space here and there when you are laying stones or brick, fill it with soil, and tuck in a tiny plant. Stones absorb the first warmth of spring, giving plants a head start. Throughout the rest of the year, they protect the roots from extreme heat and cold and eliminate any competition.

On a terrace, it's possible to space the plants more widely and avoid stepping on every plant. This affords other options, such as dwarf lady's mantle, chives, pinks, and other low-growers.

Use herbs sparingly in a path or terrace, so that the effect is natural. The plants will spread and even reseed themselves in any hint of a crack, so cut them back when they threaten to take over.

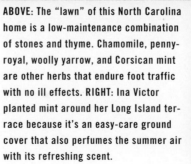

ABOVE: The "lawn" of this North Carolina home is a low-maintenance combination of stones and thyme. Chamomile, pennyroyal, woolly yarrow, and Corsican mint are other herbs that endure foot traffic with no ill effects. **RIGHT:** Ina Victor planted mint around her Long Island terrace because it's an easy-care ground cover that also perfumes the summer air with its refreshing scent.

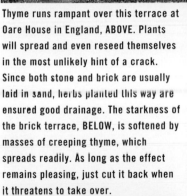

ABOVE: Woolly yarrow is used as ground cover under a bay tree at the Getty Museum in Santa Monica. RIGHT: At Linda Barksdale's lakeside home in the Northwest a mat of woolly thyme, both attractive and easy to maintain, is the focal point of a formal section of the garden. BELOW: At the Herbfarm in Seattle, the various creeping thymes surrounding a small brick square are more colorful than any pathway.

Thyme runs rampant over this terrace at Oare House in England, ABOVE. Plants will spread and even reseed themselves in the most unlikely hint of a crack. Since both stone and brick are usually laid in sand, herbs planted this way are ensured good drainage. The starkness of the brick terrace, BELOW, is softened by masses of creeping thyme, which spreads readily. As long as the effect remains pleasing, just cut it back when it threatens to take over.

When Sandra Hogan decided she wanted an herb garden at her Connecticut home, the most obvious spot for it was the big open area between the house and garage. Originally an asphalt drive that the Hogans had tried, unsuccessfully, to cover with sod, it was an unlikely spot, but the charming oasis there now is proof that with enough determination, you can create a garden anywhere.

A LABOR of love

During the eighteen years John Dallas taught landscaping at Napa College in California he nurtured the incredible rose garden that surrounds his house in the Napa Valley. Now retired, he devotes most of his time to the more than five hundred varieties that grow there, occupying every inch of yard space. This extraordinary collection of roses exists as

A PLETHORA of roses

PRECEDING PAGES: An arbor supports a variety of climbers such as Royal Sunset and Handel, both of which were developed in the 1960s, LEFT. RIGHT: The richly colored ruffled blossom of Conrad O'Neil, a shrub rose developed in 1966. THIS PAGE: Sweeps of self-sown, bright orange California poppies contrast vividly with the pink and red, a hot color combination that is most appealing under the California sun.

much for the pleasure of John's many visitors as for his own. "I wanted people to realize there are other roses besides hybrid teas," he says, "and to show them how you can use roses in landscaping." As you walk through the garden it becomes very clear just how many ways one or more of these beautiful bushes can be incorporated in any garden.

John propagates cuttings from many of his plants and sells them to visitors from a small nursery near the drive. "The best time to take a cutting," he advises, "is just after the plant has bloomed. Take it from near the center on semihard wood. Later cuttings are best done from hard wood." Occasionally neighboring roses cross-pollinate, producing an entirely new variety which John is likely to name for a grandchild.

Pruning this many roses isn't too much of a chore for someone who loves the plants as much as John does. He follows the basic rule of pruning continuous-blooming roses early in the season before bloom starts, while those with a single blooming period are pruned after blooming. In cold climates where bushes often die back in the winter, however, dead wood will have to be pruned from the single-blooming variety before bloom. It's also wise where winters are harsh to protect the roots with boughs or earth mounded up around the plant to a height of 1 foot.

Although many people believe roses require an inordinate amount of care, John insists they do not. "Roses are actually quite drought-resistant," he claims. "They could get along with only the water from the rain, but they are healthier and bloom better when they are watered regularly." Since the Napa Valley has long periods without rain, John has installed a modified drip system on a timer. Keeping the water confined to the roots is ecologically prudent and helps the leaves avoid black spot as well. He does feed the plants with a slow-release fertilizer, but "only infrequently." And there is no spraying. "I don't look at the problems, I look at the flowers," he says.

ABOVE: Bush roses such as these can be used in deep borders, as a freestanding specimen, or planted in close proximity to form a flowering hedge. Low-growing roses such as The Fairy, RIGHT, are attractive at the front of a border and useful for edging a path.

A symbol of romance, roses are also among the most versatile plants in the garden. There are shrub roses to grow in borders or as specimens and others that grow thick enough to form a hedge. Ramblers spread across fences and buildings, climbers stretch up through trees and over walls, arbors, and pergolas. Even the ground can be a bed of roses with low-growing, spreading varieties or ramblers left to run over the ground instead of on a fence. And, of course, elegant hybrid tea roses grow gloriously in a formal rose garden.

ROSE GARDENS

TOP: Shrub roses flower profusely along one side of a border at Bundels in Devon, England, where Donald Softley has collected a wide variety of roses. Lavender makes a handsome underplanting for a standard rose in this English garden, ABOVE. The profuse blooms of robust Complicata roses are used to advantage in the double border at Bourton House in Gloucestershire, RIGHT.

NEAR LEFT: At Parc Floral des Moutiers in France, white roses fill the boxwood parterres. **ABOVE:** A Frensham rose from Fitz House. **RIGHT:** In the Parc Floral des Moutiers, pink Ballerina roses share the beds in front of the rose-covered arbors with lavender and rosemary.

ABOVE RIGHT: On the terrace at Little Bowden in Berkshire, England, brilliant Red Hamburg roses grow in box-edged beds. **RIGHT:** White roses grow over tuteurs among the foxgloves in the white garden at Garden Valley Ranch in California. All climbing roses must be trained by tying them to a support, and dead wood must be pruned out. **LEFT:** Roses are trained over a wooden arbor at Polesden-Lacey in Surrey, England.

Old garden roses, those in cultivation before 1867, whose fragrant blooms range from single flowers to many-petaled rosettes, have an amazing resistance to disease and neglect. Occasionally, you can still find one growing around an old country house, but with the development of the hybrid tea in the late 1800s, these simple roses all but disappeared because their sprawling shapes and limited bloom time didn't suit formal Victorian rose gardens. Because they are easier to care for and have better fragrance and more interesting flowers than hybrid teas, old roses have regained some of their previous popularity. Many thrive with no pruning at all, but most benefit from the removal of weak or dead canes or any that are ruining the bush's shape.

Cuttings, old enough to be stiff and strong but not wooden, should be taken after the rose blooms. If you aren't going to

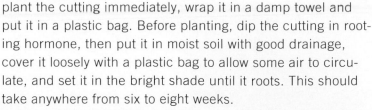

LEFT: In the Edwardian rose garden at Polesden-Lacey in Surrey, England, period and modern roses clamber over wooden pergolas. BELOW: A combination of climbing and bedded roses provides a handsome background for a cement urn at Folly Farm in Berkshire, England.

plant the cutting immediately, wrap it in a damp towel and put it in a plastic bag. Before planting, dip the cutting in rooting hormone, then put it in moist soil with good drainage, cover it loosely with a plastic bag to allow some air to circulate, and set it in the bright shade until it roots. This should take anywhere from six to eight weeks.

For years, hybrid teas have been the most popular garden rose. Although not always fragrant, they are reliable repeat flowerers. These roses do best when treated to manure or compost along with fertilizer in the first spring feeding and in the one following the first flowering. Prune first-year plants back to 6 inches; cut older plants back to 12 inches and remove all weak and dead wood. If you want perfect roses with no mildew or black spot, you will have to use a spray.

The newest roses are those developed by the British rosarian David Austin. They combine the striking flowers, incredible fragrance, and heartiness of the old shrub roses with the continuous bloom of modern cultivars. Available in sizes to fit any garden, they are perfect for landscaping or mixing with perennials in borders. For bigger blooms, cut the plants back hard in the early spring, leaving just a few canes.

Much of the beauty of rambling roses, like those that adorn a brick wall at Littlecote in England, LEFT, comes from the lovely curving arcs of the canes. When one dies out, it is cut all the way back to the base to maintain the line. ABOVE: Roses grow on a simple wooden support at Bundels.

The canes of ramblers are so flexible they are easily espaliered, like those that grow against the house in the courtyard at Bourton House, RIGHT. BELOW: Roses climb over the door of a cottage.

RIGHT: A mixture of red and white roses climbs over the railing of the terrace at Little Bowden. BOTTOM, FAR LEFT: A tree becomes a living support for climbing roses, whose blossoms eventually peek through the leaves in a display of color. BELOW LEFT: Belle Story, one of David Austin's roses.

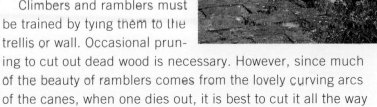

Climbers and ramblers must be trained by tying them to the trellis or wall. Occasional pruning to cut out dead wood is necessary. However, since much of the beauty of ramblers comes from the lovely curving arcs of the canes, when one dies out, it is best to cut it all the way back to the base to maintain the line.

All roses should be planted in rich organic soil with good drainage and fertilized monthly from spring through the beginning of August. Keep them well watered, preferably with soaker hoses to avoid wet leaves that can lead to black spot. Leaving enough room around the plants for good air circulation also discourages fungal diseases. In severely cold climates, roses will probably need some winter protection. Mound earth around bushes to a height of 1 foot to protect the roots. Tree roses should be tipped over parallel to the ground and covered with earth, while climbers should be taken off their supports, tied around a tall support, then wrapped in straw and burlap and the roots covered with soil.

california
GARDENING

The McDuffies came to Montecito

in search of land on which to keep a

cherished Morgan horse. Seeing these

fields overlooking the mountains, they

knew they had found their spot. "My

father-in-law used a tractor to level the

fields and we built a barn," says Mary

McDuffie. "There was no house, but I'm

a compulsive planter so the first garden

was around the barn."

The house they eventually built was small and so was the garden around it. Then six years ago the McDuffies undertook a major renovation, enlarging both house and garden. The bones of the present garden were established with the help of Isabelle Greene, a garden designer known for her ecologically sensitive plantings. "We concentrated on indigenous plant material. After all, plants are happiest in their own environments," notes Mrs. McDuffie. Because water is in short supply in the area, the garden was designed to be drought-tolerant, surviving with minimum watering when necessary. When the wells are full, more generous watering is possible and trees, particularly, are given deep waterings to make up for the lean times. Grass, which requires massive amounts of water, is kept to the barest minimum.

"Water-conscious planting doesn't mean the gardens have to be colorless," notes Mrs. McDuffie. "I love the drama of walking out and seeing the white and blue of campanula coming through the chartreuse flowers of lady's mantle." Lashings of annuals add more excitement and color. Partial to soft colors like those in the distant mountains, Mrs. McDuffie even grows apricot foxgloves instead of the more common "harsh raspberry" variety.

Plants that don't do well, like chamomile, are given several chances, then replaced by others. "A garden can't be a set piece. It would have no life. And experimentation is half the fun of gardening," she says. Herbs are worked in with the flowers and vegetables. "My theory is that as long as you're satisfied with the results you can do what you want. You don't have to follow

PRECEDING PAGES: Gracefully curved paths, LEFT, soften the garden. The trellis at the far end provides a backdrop for the vegetable garden and lends structure to the wide open spaces. A thyme-covered stone path, RIGHT, threads its way through the plantings. THIS PAGE: Woolly yarrow encircles a sundial in the kitchen garden, which is housed in a series of raised beds. A Belgian fence of espaliered apple trees, a reminder of Mrs. McDuffie's ancestral home in France, borders one side.

Mrs. McDuffie enjoys using ancient objects and old stones as decorative focal points in the garden, often combining several, like the old oil jars, OPPOSITE, for greatest impact. Poppies and other annuals are scattered throughout the garden to add color, LEFT. The muted colors of the distant mountains are reflected in this garden, BELOW, mellowed even further by drought-resistant gray foliage plants such as lamb's ears.

a set of rules," she adds. But Mrs. McDuffie is adamant about how important it is to prepare the soil well. All the beds were originally double-dug, a process that involves removing a spadeful of earth and setting it at the far end of the bed. Then a spadeful of compost or manure is dug into the next layer of soil, and the top spadeful of earth from the next section of the bed is shoveled on top. This process continues down the bed until you reach the end, where the first spadeful of earth is used to complete the job. Now the beds are fed each year with homemade compost enriched with the manure from their horses.

In the kitchen garden, vegetables are planted in patterns for the sheer pleasure of it. Lettuces of every kind abound since Mr. McDuffie is "the original Mr. McGregor, mad about lettuce." While daytime temperatures are high, cool evenings enable the lettuces to survive. Because planting space here is limited and it is difficult to rotate crops, a ground cover of vetch is planted each fall and incorporated into the soil in the spring to add nutrients.

"The garden absorbs a great amount of time," admits Mrs. McDuffie, "but it's our refuge. It's always peaceful and serene; stress ebbs away and your spirit is restored."

When he decided to redo the gardens around his California house, William Slater wanted to ensure that they would look attractive even when threatened by water shortages. The resulting landscape, which relies heavily on herbs such as yarrow, santolina, and lavender, is a splendid example of a garden that is lush and colorful and yet still ecologically correct.

A DROUGHT-TOLERANT garden

Born of ecological concerns, Xeriscaping is a relatively new gardening discipline embraced most eagerly in areas where water is scarce and ongoing droughts have forced gardeners to rethink their methods. The basic premise is to garden close to nature, using plants native to the area that can survive without gallons of additional, often unavailable, water and with the use of few or no pesticides.

XERISCAPING

Santolina and rosemary are among the herbs suitable for water-conserving gardens, **TOP LEFT**. The field of lavender at Bernard Perris's Provençal *mas*, **ABOVE**, thrives in the hot dry summers of Provence and is a colorful alternative to a water-greedy lawn. Lavender requires little care as long as it has good drainage and sun, but it will not grow well where humidity is high or there is a great deal of rain. At Carole Rosenberg's Long Island home, **LEFT**, yarrow, lavender, and a variety of grasses have been used to create a lush natural garden that requires little water.

LEFT: The many varieties of sage work well in natural water-restricted gardens and provide a range of flowers and foliage. RIGHT: Xeriscaping was an important consideration when Mark Brown planned this orchard in Normandy. Grass paths tame what would otherwise be a meadow of wildflowers and grasses requiring little water or care.

Herbs, especially those with silver foliage, play an important role in this kind of gardening, as the juxtaposition of different-colored foliage replaces some of the color interest normally achieved with flowers. Most silvery plants, natives of hot, dry Mediterranean climates, get their color from tiny hairs on the leaves, which diffuse and reflect sunlight, reducing the amount of water lost to evaporation. And since they like the heat, the more sun they get, the healthier (and hairier) they become, making them even paler in color. Mediterranean natives such as thyme, rosemary, lavender, savory, curry plant, and lamb's ears actually prefer dry soil and thrive under hot sun. Coneflower, Joe-Pye weed, and goldenrod, herbal wildflowers that readily survive unattended in fields, are some alternatives to more demanding perennials.

While choosing the proper plants for the climate and soil is the first step in Xeriscaping, designing the garden is equally important. Moisture-greedy lawns can be replaced with large sweeps of less thirsty plants like thyme or sedum; "rivers" made of pebbles or stones can run through the garden to add interest; and native flowers can predominate. Shun showy fountains whose spray dissipates water.

Xeriscaping does not eliminate watering but does aim to save water and use it the most efficient way. Drip irrigation systems minimize evaporation and make it easier to tailor the watering of different sections of a garden, allowing a bit more water for the occasional special plant. Heavy mulching prevents rapid evaporation, holding any available moisture from nature or a drip irrigation system in the ground longer. Natural mulches may even provide enough moisture for certain plants: woodruff, for example, will absorb the moisture of the composted leaves of the tree under which it is growing.

ABOVE: The path leading from the inn down to the water at Sooke Harbour House on Vancouver Island is lined with masses of wild roses and with fennel that constantly reseeds itself.

A family GARDEN

Rosalind Cameron is no stranger to the garden at East Kennett Manor, a house in Wiltshire she first visited as a child fleeing wartime London. About twenty years ago she returned with her husband to live here full-time. Since then she has simplified the garden. "Most of the shrubs and hedges were planted by my mother," she says, "but I have changed the garden gradually

THE SILVER HERBS

ABOVE: Susan Ryley uses silvery mullein, lamb's ears, and artemisia to brighten a shady Vancouver border. LEFT: Lamb's ears contrast handsomely with catnip and soften the vivid hues in this California border created by Foxglove Designs, BOTTOM LEFT, and focus attention on the amillary sundial in Nancy Walz's Maryland herb garden, BELOW.

The beautiful silver-gray foliage of herbs such as lamb's ears, santolina, lavender, sage, and the artemisias is one of the gardener's most valuable design tools. These pungent plants, whose colors range from almost white to a steely blue-gray, may have some pretty blossoms of their own, but it is the varied texture of their foliage, from the broad, furry leaves of lamb's ears to the fine spikes of lavender, that is so prized by gardeners. They bring a welcome diversity to the greens when flowers are scarce.

Perhaps the greatest asset of these plants, however, is the

Nancy Goslee Powers uses drought-resistant silver-foliage plants for both their practicality and their suitability for her Mediterranean-style California garden, BELOW. In the easy-care formal landscape she designed, RIGHT, the visual impact comes from the contrast of silvery santolina with dark green yew. The same handsome contrast works as well when rosemary and santolina tumble over a wall, CENTER RIGHT. BOTTOM RIGHT: Lamb's ears add their silvery glow to the silver-and-white garden at Hascombe Court in Surrey.

way their silvery neutrality instills harmony and visual unity in the garden, softening and calming masses of contrasting colors and helping the gardener segue from one color palette to another without clashing. At the same time, they enhance an especially bright flower planted nearby far better than their green-leaved neighbors. They are also an essential part of an all-white garden.

Because they reflect light, silver herbs also give the garden a luminous quality even on dreary days, and can be used to brighten up dark corners. The faintest glimmer of moonlight illuminates a path lined with lamb's ears, and without their foliage, it would be a difficult task to design a "moon" garden, that combination of white pebble paths, bright white flowers, and silver plants that is such an enchanting sight under soft lunar rays.

Since many of these plants are native to the Mediterranean region, and best suited to hot, dry climates, grow them in a sunny spot with excellent drainage and mulch them when temperatures dip below freezing.

For fifteen years Carol and Jack Kelly had a horse pasture for a front yard; the only garden was a bit of nondescript landscaping around the house. "I wanted a garden, but I didn't know where to begin," says Carol. "With no background in gardening, I made a lot of false starts. Then we took a trip to Mount Vernon and I learned from that garden how to control a big space by

A
GARDEN IN THE
northwest

PRECEDING PAGES: Jack Kelly built the greenhouse, LEFT, relatively inexpensively by using recycled windows and remnants of filigree from Victorian houses. Although wood requires more maintenance than metal, appearance was more important to Carol because the structure is situated in the front garden. An armillary sundial surrounded by santolina is the focal point, RIGHT, of this garden "room." THIS PAGE: Trellised roses and birdhouses both decorate and camouflage an unfortunately situated telephone pole in this garden "room," BELOW. Carol calls it her "tenement" for sparrows, starlings, and other indiscriminate birds. RIGHT: Pale pink Heritage roses are enclosed by low box hedges in another garden room. Cécile Brunner and deep red Grootendorst Supreme roses, foxglove, lavender, yarrow, and lupins are among the other plants that border the central geometric design.

dividing it into small 'rooms.'" For Carol, an inveterate decorator, this new vantage point helped crystallize her garden plan.

Since the field had once been a riverbed, the Kellys had the tedious job of removing the rocky residue. Double-digging and enriching the soil before planting was the most important step, though, because once the perennials were in place it would have been difficult to amend the soil without digging out all the plants.

The soil tends toward clay, so Carol continues to work on it by mulching all the beds with 2 inches of homemade compost every fall to keep it friable. "And I always carry a pail of compost, sand, chicken manure, and bonemeal when I'm planting so that I can dig some in around new plants," she says.

Carol's first garden was a structured series of garden rooms. Once the basic divisions were laid out and the beds installed, boxwood hedges were planted to help define the plan. Since the ivy-covered well house was already in place, the Kellys built a grape-covered gazebo for balance. After the beds were filled with a variety of herbs and perennials, Carol set her sights on the open land across the drive.

"I was more daring on this side because I was more secure," she admits. "There are more curvy lines here, and I'm still experimenting with the planting. I want to include more shrubs for their colored foliage and to give the garden more height and year-round interest."

Throughout, stone birds, birdhouses, jugs, and other decorations add humor and personality to the garden. "I like to surprise people, to add a little whimsy," she says. "Although you should have a plan for your plants, you shouldn't have one for the decorations. If you love something, it will work. Just don't overdo it: in a small garden especially, you have to be very selective. After all, a garden is really for the plants."

Roses, delphinium, lamb's ears, perennial geraniums, foxglove, and lady's mantle are among the plants bordering the fence that separates the garden room from the rest of the garden, OPPOSITE. The gazebo is covered with grapevines, while roses climb the arbor. TOP AND ABOVE: Birds, both real and decorative, abound in the Kellys' garden. A "blackbird" perches on a stone pedestal, while a "dove" rests on a terra-cotta column.

GARDEN STRUCTURES

LEFT: Elaine Burden uses a lattice fence to divide her Virginia garden into separate sections and a rose-covered arbor as a transition between them. **ABOVE:** At Kerdaloo in France, Prince Wolkonsky decorated the inside of his garden shelters with fanciful mosaics of shells.

LEFT: The arbor leading to Wendy Lauderdale's front door in Wiltshire, England, is covered with pink Comte de Chambord roses and white Rosa Cerasocarpa and underplanted with catmint. **RIGHT:** A charming gazebo with a built-in seat all around provides a shady spot in which to relax on a Long Island horse farm.

Whether it's a small outbuilding, a greenhouse, or simply a traditional arbor or rose pillar, a garden structure helps establish both the plan and the character of a garden, and often gives plants another place to grow. Like other elements, it should be harmonious with the garden's style.

The simplest of all garden structures is the rose pillar or the rose pyramid, used on its own or in the middle of a border to support roses or other climbing plants. A metal trainer shaped like an umbrella is another, more formal version. All add height and shape to the garden and show plants to their greatest advantage. Although traditional models are of metal or carefully crafted lattice, simple bamboo stakes or twigs that have been nailed or tied together work equally well in an informal garden.

Arbors are among the most popular garden structures. They can lead to a secret spot, provide an attractive transition from

LEFT: In an informal part of his Oregon garden, Wallace Huntington used three wooden stakes to create a simple support for climbing roses. He built his gazebo, BELOW, with carefully crafted lattice. BOTTOM: At Brook Lodge Farm Cottage in Surrey, a bench set in a charming windowed shelter allows Mrs. Kingham to sit in her garden even on cool or rainy days.

BELOW: Simple wooden rose pillars add structure to Jane Rivkin's garden. The sheltered garden bench is a focal point for the path.

ABOVE: This rose garden in Estacada, Oregon, is enclosed with a rose-covered lattice-work wall. Built-in niches display a collection of garden statuary. ABOVE RIGHT: The lattice rose pillars at Pound Hill House in England are constructed in an unusual X-shaped configuration. A formal box garden is enhanced by a small outbuilding on Elaine Burden's Virginia farm, BELOW.

one part of the garden to another, or even be freestanding when used as a focal point or a place to grow a special rose. Whether arched or squared off, arbors are traditionally covered with climbing roses, clematis, or other flowering vines. Always available in wood and metal, they are now also being made in heavy white plastic, a practical option as they never rot or need paint.

Closely related to arbors, pergolas are generally designed to provide a transition from one place to another, but they can also stand on their own near a pool or around a rose garden, for example, to lend importance to what they frame. When covered with fragrant roses or other climbing plants such as wisteria, they provide welcome shade for a garden walk or, if they are wide enough to hold a bench, a cool place to sit and read. Although they can have a lovely curving shape, they are more often straight. Natural or painted wood pergolas are most popular, but they might be of metal or have columns of stone or cement in a formal garden.

Gazebos are among the most romantic of garden structures. These small open shelters beckon you to sit in their shade on hot afternoons while soft breezes flutter through, and they offer the ideal place for afternoon tea, candlelit dinners on warm evenings, or a secret tryst. Whether an ornate Victorian style or a rustic structure built of twigs, a gazebo should be chosen to complement your house and garden. Since it is a major structure, select its site carefully to avoid overwhelming any part of the garden or crowding another building. It should also catch the breezes and have a nice view.

Any small building, whether a toolshed or a greenhouse, can be used to add mass to a garden with few trees and shrubs, and serve as a focal point around which to plant a garden. It can also obscure a bad view. Placed at the end of the garden, a building draws the eye along the border, and when it is nestled among the trees, it has the feeling of a private refuge. The architecture of the building might be simple and cottagelike or have the rich fantasy of an English folly—the choice is yours.

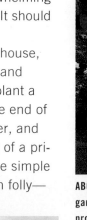

ABOVE: In Charlotte Moss's Long Island garden, the pool house has been sited to provide a framework for the pool and its surrounding rose garden. **LEFT:** In Virginia's open fields, Abe Pollin defined his herb garden with fencing and an open pergola that incorporates a gazebo as a passageway. **RIGHT:** A gazebo at Jenkyn Place in Hampshire, England, is partially enclosed to provide support for a built-in bench. **BELOW:** An elegant wooden structure supporting pleached trees forms the cool green arcade demarcating the perimeter of a garden at Het Loo Palace in Holland.

LEFT: Once the roses have completely covered this open metal structure at the Herbfarm in Seattle, it becomes a shady bower for conversation or tea. **ABOVE:** Freestanding terra-cotta pillars and pergolas frame a view of the Moroccan mountains at La Rosarie near Marrakesh.

When Lani Freymiller planned her California garden, she avoided a symmetrical layout because she believes that nothing in nature is symmetrical. This is a very personal garden, actually a series of gardens, designed by Lani herself, and although the overall plan may not be symmetrical, the planting areas, filled with herbs and flowers in the hot colors she loves, do have a sense of order. Situated

A HIDDEN garden

WALLS, FENCES, AND GATES

Walls are an invaluable element of garden design. They can be used to divide a large uninteresting space into more intimate areas, to enclose the entire garden and protect it from the street and neighbors, to terrace steep hills, to screen out unsightly areas, or simply to focus attention on a passageway. Permanent walls can be constructed of brick, stone, cement, or stucco. Although they can be left bare, they are especially handsome when softened with climbing roses, ivy, hops, or espaliered fruit trees.

ABOVE LEFT: Silvery artemisia provides a nice contrast to Sue Litt's black iron Victorian fence. **ABOVE:** The graceful shape of a wooden gate in Ryan Gainey's Atlanta garden lends it a certain formality that complements the statuary-topped brick pillars. This is an example of a gate designed to contrast with, rather than echo the material of the wall. **LEFT:** A wall of roses grows atop a stone retaining wall at Jenkyn Place in Hampshire, England.

ABOVE: A tiered stucco wall allows room for planting on different levels. Prostrate rosemary crawls over the lower section. RIGHT: Rhubarb forcers and terra-cotta pots are stacked against the old stone wall around a working courtyard at Bourton House in Gloucestershire, England. BELOW: At Lower Severalls in Somerset, England, two imposing stone columns anchor a simple iron gate.

ABOVE: Stacked firewood disguises a basic barbed-wire fence. BELOW: A gate is needed to provide access when walls, fences, or hedges enclose an area. Here, an iron grille door is set into a brick wall overrun with roses.

ABOVE: The handsome old wall that once surrounded the Victorian kitchen garden at the Round House in Surrey is an interesting combination of brick and stone. RIGHT: A stone retaining wall creates a spot to plant herbs in Marge Haller's Ohio garden. BELOW: A white picket fence covered with roses is a classic enclosure for a cottage garden.

ABOVE: At Folly Farm in Berkshire, England, a decorative wooden gate provides access to the garden through a brick wall. BELOW: A *clairvoyée* in a brick wall at Polesden-Lacy offers strollers on the far side an enticing glimpse of the inner gardens.

The retaining walls required to support terraces on sloping terrain are frequently built of simple railroad ties, but stones, mortared or unmortared, are equally practical and often more decorative. If you choose the latter, the wall can be pressed into service as a form of rock garden.

Fences, both practical and decorative, serve many of the same purposes as walls, as do hedges. Traditionally fences were used to define property lines, keeping strangers out and children and animals in, but they also give a garden structure, ensure privacy, and protect tender plants from chill winds. Rustic logs or specially shaped pickets, stalks of bamboo, or intricately molded metal are some of the most popular fencing materials.

Solid walls and fences are a plus when you want to screen out the street, a neighbor, or an unsightly structure. And

ABOVE: A neat white wooden lattice fence, more formal in feeling than the usual picket, encloses the Slaymakers' Nashville garden in an airy way. The matching lattice gate is functional without being disruptive. RIGHT: In Ohio, Pat Beckman uses a rustic wooden fence to separate the field-grown plants from the rest of the garden. Wide pickets strengthen the gate.

TOP: Jean Mus used stone retaining walls to create a terraced garden on a steep Provençal hillside. ABOVE: Thyme tumbles over the slope above this retaining wall in Marge Haller's garden.

while they are useful in blocking strong winds, they also inhibit breezes on warm summer days, so use them with care around hot-weather seating areas. Open stonework, slats, lattice, or a hedge might be a better alternative.

Available in a range of materials and styles, walls and fences should be chosen for their compatibility with both house and garden. In general, wood and stone tend to be more rustic than metal and brick, but the actual style of the wall or fence can influence the final effect as much as the material does.

When walls, fences, or hedges enclose an area, a gate is often needed to provide access. Gates in fences are most often made of the same material as the fence, but there are

FAR LEFT: A tall hedge underplanted with herbs walls off one section of the garden at Jenkyn Place in Hampshire, England. ABOVE: Dulcey Mahar uses box hedges to accentuate the pathways in her Portland, Oregon, garden. LEFT: Rosemary surrounds a weathered picket fence in the Napa Valley in California. BOTTOM LEFT: At this Long Island horse farm, the post-and-rail fence enclosing a horse pasture is softened with roses and catmint. BELOW: A cheerful carved bird adorns the wooden gate to Ruth Warner's Nashville garden.

LEFT: Herbs suchs as sage, marjoram, rosemary, and thyme growing robustly in an unmortared stone retaining wall at Sandy Mush Nursery create an impromptu rock garden.

times when a departure seems more interesting. Both wood and metal gates are suitable for brick and stone walls as long as they reflect the style of the wall and the garden.

The width of the gate will vary according to space and use, but should never be less than 3 feet for comfortable access. If the gate will also be used for a mower or other lawn equipment, make sure the opening is large enough to accommodate the machinery.

ABOVE: A post-and-rail fence is a suitable choice for this informal herb garden at Barn Owl Nursery in Oregon. LEFT: Jim and Susan Pollack used rock walls to terrace a slope in their Northwest garden, then planted it with a colorful array of herbs and flowers.

THE round HOUSE

In Victorian times, the duke of

Westminster reigned over a large Surrey

estate with a handsome walled vegetable

garden. In one corner of the garden there

was a charming round house that was home

to the nine gardeners and four gamekeepers

who watched over the grounds. Death duties

forced the duke's family to break up and sell

the property, and now the Round House is

home to Vivian and Heather Taylor, who

As a child, John Musnicki hated garden-

ing because he had to earn his allowance by

weeding. However, walking through his

Bridgehampton, Long Island, garden today,

it's apparent that despite a bad start he's a

born gardener who revels in exploring and

nurturing a wide variety of plant mate-

rial. After a career that has

included estate gardening

and establishing

A
LANDSCAPER'S
garden

a nursery, John has settled into a landscaping business that allows him to spend many hours in the fields during the growing season, experimenting with wildflowers, iris, and other flowers and shrubs.

The garden around his house began taking shape when he bought some dwarf conifers from a collection being sold off by an estate. After he got them home, planting beds had to be laid out. "I don't like straight lines," he says, "so I drove my lawn mower around the lawn, making nice curves." Since the lawn mower designed the curves, they are easy to follow when it's time to cut the grass. Once John had established the shape of the beds, he employed a sod cutter to remove the sod. The soil was cultivated, then fertilized with 50 percent organic 10/6/4 fertilizer, which is not harsh

PRECEDING PAGES: Masses of lavender edge the border in front of a carefully refurbished 100-year-old fence from nearby Southampton, LEFT. Lavender edges the curving brick path near the herb garden, RIGHT. The decorative old stone marker doubles as a hose guide. THIS PAGE: A circular herb garden outside the kitchen door, LEFT, is centered on a handsome stone sundial. The curving brick paths that thread through the garden were laid over those created in the dirt by the natural flow of foot traffic. The bricks are set in just enough sand to anchor them, and the width of the path varies according to the site. Visitors to the house are welcomed by an old bench framed in everblooming Fairy roses, ABOVE.

PRECEDING PAGES: Winding dirt paths lead through a mixture of colorful flowers and herbs, LEFT. In a curve of the path, RIGHT, stones set among creeping thyme lead to a stone bench framed in lamb's ears. THIS PAGE: The sloping land in the front garden has been terraced with railroad ties, LEFT, which were also used for steps between the different levels. ABOVE: As paths meander through the garden, gray foliage plants and white blossoms draw the eye along while providing a pleasant contrast to the many pinks and purples. A large boulder acts as a garden ornament.

and Judy began propagating and selling them. Profits financed another garden in front of the house and enabled her to give up her day job.

In planning her garden, Judy sought a natural look. "I wanted it to seem as if you might be walking through a field of wildflowers," she explains. She was attracted to herbs from the beginning because they provided the right color balance and a wide variety of texture and foliage. "The silvery gray foliage of artemisia and salvia make the color of flowers like penstemon pop," she notes. "And they help break up the greens. That's particularly important with perennials." She has since discovered that herbs also help keep her garden healthy by repelling certain insects.

The garden is cleverly laid out so that the eye doesn't take it all in at once. Since the ground was flat, Judy devised hidden places with flowering shrubs. Paths meander through these sheltered spots, and benches are thoughtfully placed to

LEFT: Lavender surrounded by alstomeria and isotoma axilaris, a ground cover native to Australia, creates a colorful vignette. As the paths wind through the garden, curves and carefully sited shrubs hide the plantings that lie ahead, creating a sense of discovery, RIGHT.

invite visitors to sit and admire the flowers.

Judy has very definite opinions on how to plant a garden. "To learn the character of a plant, you must have it in the garden for at least a year. You should base your plan on hot or cool colors: choose one or the other. Using one color predominately makes the garden look larger, and there is no interruption of the peaceful flow of color."

Once she had planned the structure of the garden, Judy began planting. "I collected many plants, then planted on a day when my mind was clear. It takes a certain amount of concentration," she adds. Bold foliage is planted near delicate leaves for contrast. Many plants in the garden are natives of South Africa and Australia; they thrive in California because the climates are quite similar. Shrubs act as a backdrop all around the garden, and different-sized plants are arranged to make peepholes affording enticing glimpses of the rest of the garden. Once the garden is planted, it requires constant observation and care. "If something disturbs you where it is, take it out and move it," Judy advises.

EDGINGS

It is both practical and decorative to use some kind of edging in an herb garden. Without them, grass creeps from the lawn or path into the beds, fighting with the plants for nutrients and space and making the chore of weeding more difficult. They also eliminate the job of edging the beds with a spade several times a season. And where beds border on gravel or wood-chip paths, edgings prevent the plants from roaming into the paths.

TOP RIGHT AND ABOVE: Strips of flexible bender board secured with wooden builder's stakes are a good solution for edging curved beds like these at Barn Owl Nursery in Oregon. At Manor Farm in Wiltshire, England, catmint edges the lawn, RIGHT. Treated boards, FAR RIGHT, are a simple, practical, and appropriate edging for an informal garden.

While it is practical to use steel or plastic strips from the garden center to edge a bed, decorative edgings can be just as effective and far more charming. They also help to define the style and plan of the garden visually. Brick is one popular edging, especially handsome when set on end at an angle to make a jagged border. Belgian block also works well, and antique Victorian edging tiles are now being reproduced. Other decorative edgings like stones or low wattle fencing are not as effective in restraining the grass but make up for their lack of practicality in charm.

In a more informal garden, railroad ties are a satisfactory if somewhat less decorative solution, and in addition to defining the planting space, they form a raised bed, which improves drainage and makes soil improvement easier.

One of the easiest ways to edge an herb garden is simply with more herbs. Spilling naturally over the edges, they soften the hard lines of a stone or brick path and lessen the need to edge a grass one. Lamb's ears, catnip, lavender, lady's mantle, lemon balm, scented geraniums, and others with a spreading growth habit are among the best edging plants.

A double row of stones is a complementary edging for a pebble path, ABOVE. Ryan Gainey creates a whimsical edging with upside-down flower pots, BELOW. At the Herbfarm, local stones outline the beds, RIGHT. Karen Cauble uses stripped logs, MIDDLE RIGHT, to define the beds in her herb garden. BELOW RIGHT: In Morocco's Majoral Gardens, bright blue cement curbing contrasts handsomely with greenery and vivid flowers like nasturtiums.

Folk artist James Cramer has cre-

ated an extremely idiosyncratic garden

around the old Maryland farmhouse he

shares with fellow folk artist Dean Johnson.

The garden is filled with the carefully

crafted birdhouses that are Dean's

specialty as well as with rustic

antiques leading a second

life in the garden.

A
FOLK ARTIST'S
garden

PRECEDING PAGES, LEFT: The focal point of the kitchen garden is an old pump. Jimmie displays his collection of old baskets and bunches of dried herbs near the old washhouse fireplace, RIGHT. THIS PAGE, LEFT AND OPPOSITE: In the seating area Dean's fanciful scarecrow bench accommodates more guests. An old trestle table serves as a potting bench. A handmade "heart" gate marks the entrance to the garden. Dean built the log-cabin birdhouse, RIGHT, complete with picket fence.

When the two moved in, the only existing plants were a white hydrangea, a rose, and a grapevine supported by an old piece of wood. Working on the garden himself, Jimmie tackled one area at a time. "It's easier if you can work around something that already exists," he says. "Since we had these rocks with some sort of well in them just outside the kitchen door, I started there. We found an old pump to act as a focal point and added on."

Once they had the pump in place, Jimmie planted a circular garden around it. The first step, of course, was to prepare the soil by adding chicken manure, peat moss, and composted grass. Planned as a kitchen garden, this space was filled with culinary herbs. "Although I don't have time to cook because I'm too busy gardening and working, I like making

LEFT: A bee skep is protected from the elements by an old feed scoop turned upside down and supported on four legs. OPPOSITE: As Jimmie expanded the garden, he created a seating area next to an old washhouse that now doubles as a handy garden shed. OVERLEAF: An overall view of the garden.

potpourri and decorating with dried flowers. Sometimes I'll just put a big bowl of orange mint in the house for the nice fresh smell," says Jimmie.

The stone walkway, too, was already in place and herbs soon grew along the edges. "I was very aware of colors and textures when I planted along the walkway," says Jimmie. "The idea of lamb's ears with their furry gray leaves spilling over the path excited me. It's important to add variety to the planting by varying the heights of the plants," he adds, so sage, oregano, and tansy among others were layered along the paths as well as in front of an existing fence. Each year since then, the garden has been expanded. After planting along the fence on the property line, Jimmie created a garden in one corner, then another in the back.

Jimmie takes care of the garden in small spurts throughout the day. "I come out in the morning and drink coffee in the herb garden. I pick a few weeds," he says. "Then I go up to the studio and work. When I take a coffee break, I do more weeds. I water in the evening and I'm out here for hours. I get carried away with creative ideas. I look around and think about what we need for the garden, like a scarecrow, then Dean builds it."

BIRDHOUSES

From their earliest incarnation as the cottage-size houses the ancient Romans built to shelter their doves and pigeons, birdhouses changed little until the late 1800s. Giant dovecotes gave way to smaller houses, far more suitable for the average garden and more appealing to the small birds that inhabited the fields.

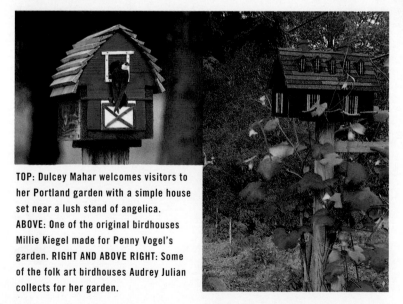

TOP: Dulcey Mahar welcomes visitors to her Portland garden with a simple house set near a lush stand of angelica. ABOVE: One of the original birdhouses Millie Kiegel made for Penny Vogel's garden. RIGHT AND ABOVE RIGHT: Some of the folk art birdhouses Audrey Julian collects for her garden.

In the years since, birdhouses have added their charm to many gardens. Often the work of folk artists, they might be replicas of familiar buildings like barns, country churches, log cabins, or even gas stations. Due to the current interest in gardening and folk art, vintage birdhouses are avidly sought after at flea markets and antiques shows by gardeners and collectors alike and can command high prices.

Birdhouses can sit atop a tall pole to draw attention to a specific area, or you can run a group of poles along a boundary fence, emphasizing the line and allowing birds easy access. Some birdhouses are designed to be hung from tree limbs, others to be attached to the side of the house or simply set on a stump or rock.

These charming abodes can be purely decorative or can

ABOVE: Ryan Gainey creates an avian town, complete with a church, in one corner of the garden. RIGHT: A big family of birds would be comfortable in Kerry Hippensteel's carefully constructed house, complete with front porch. BELOW: The dovecote from Carol Kelly's garden.

ABOVE, TOP TO BOTTOM: An impressive mansion from Audrey Julian's collection; this formal house is a splendid example of Dean Johnson's craftsmanship; a rustic house with a tin roof from Ryan Gainey's garden. LEFT: Thanks to Millie Kiegel, Penny Vogel's birds even have a general store.

The rose-covered brick dovecote at Littlecote House in Berkshire, **LEFT**. **ABOVE:** Millie Kiegel welcomes favorite birds with a heart. In Andrea Dern's California garden, lucky birds reside in a house with its own shaded porch, **BELOW**.

TOP LEFT: The dovecote at Heale House. **CENTER LEFT:** Another of Dean Johnson's contributions to Jimmie Cramer's garden. **LEFT:** Millie Kiegel's Fly Low Inn provides shelter for migrating birds. **RIGHT:** In Maryland, a more rustic group would enjoy the beautifully detailed log cabin crafted by Dean Johnson.

help shelter the many birds whose natural habitats are being destroyed as more and more land is covered with buildings. Although most birds nest in the open, there are forty species, among them purple martins, wrens, and bluebirds, that prefer the shelter of a house. To attract them, make sure your birdhouse has holes for both ventilation and drainage—and a way to clean out old nests each season so they don't become infested with parasites and mites or before wasps or mice decide to take over the space.

The interior capacity and size of the hole will determine which birds will seek shelter in your birdhouse. As a general rule, a 1½-inch hole should be large enough for most birds that might apply. A perch, although handy, is not essential.

The busy dovecote at Bernard Perris's Provençal *mas* is nestled snugly under verdant ivy, **ABOVE**. In Margaret Willoughby's Oregon garden, two birdhouses are nearly hidden by a cloud of Rambling Rector roses, **LEFT. BELOW:** Another of Millie Kiegel's birdhouses, this one from Penny Vogel's garden.

LEFT: Serena Bouanchaud provides the birds in her garden with a porch to shade them from the hot Louisiana sun.

AN herbal PARADISE

High on a sunny slope of Vancouver Island, Noel Richardson and Andrew Yeoman have turned an old farm into an herbal paradise called Raven Hill Herb Farm in honor of the ravens that swoop overhead while they garden. Andrew spent their first summer here sketching plans for the garden—and it was not until they were complete that the first plant went in. "It's important to let the garden flow from the

At first they concentrated on culinary herbs to supply fresh-cut herbs to chefs, a business they had taken over from a neighbor on impulse. For easier care and better results, Andrew was careful to plant those requiring good rich soil and those that thrive in poor soil in different beds. He fertilizes the garden with leaf mold from local oaks, chicken and sheep manure, and composted grass clippings. Bonemeal or rock phosphate and lime make up for a lack of those in the soil. "And I tend not to grow anything that presents a problem," he notes. "As a rule, herbs are more pest- and disease-free than flowers, although occasionally the nasturtiums get aphids."

Since Noel prefers the loose style of English cottage gardens to Andrew's tidy approach, they have divided the gardening chores, with Noel responsible for the containers on the patio and behind the house. These are filled with a mixture of two-thirds potting soil and one-third Andrew's compost. "I fer-

tilize them every week, and in July and August I generally have to water daily," she says. Culinary herbs grow in the back but you're likely to find lemon verbena underplanted with nasturtiums, bay and rosemary topiaries, white daisies and petunias, and whatever else may catch Noel's fancy in the pots on the patio. They spend happy summers outside, then the tender perennials go into the cold greenhouse for the winter. "They're like children after awhile," she says.

The proximity to so many fresh herbs has led Noel to a new career as a cooking teacher and cookbook author. Every edible herb and flower in the garden eventually finds its way to her kitchen and into a tantalizing dish to be shared with the chefs who buy the herbs and with visitors to the farm.

ABOVE: Many of Noel's culinary herbs are grown in barrels behind the house. The contrasting colors and textures of the thymes planted on the rock wall along the drive, OPPOSITE, create a magnificent tapestry that requires almost no maintenance.

GARDEN SEATS

A wrought iron seat encircles a tree in Anne Cox Chambers's Provençal garden, **ABOVE**. At Charlton Park in England, an intricate iron bench, **TOP RIGHT**, nestles among the pink and white flowers. Manipulating wire can result in a variety of chair designs, such as this pinwheel motif, **RIGHT**. **BELOW**: A curved and trellised wooden seat set into a hedge provides a shady retreat in the gardens at Het Loo Palace in Holland.

A garden cannot be enjoyed properly without a comfortable seat from which to sit and admire the varied foliage and dainty flowers of your favorite herbs, inhaling their heady fragrance while you watch the bees and butterflies.

The choice of garden seats is enormous, ranging from meticulous reproductions of traditional metal or wood chairs and benches to fanciful twig seats crafted by contemporary folk artists. There are benches that fit around the trunk of a shady tree, seats built into rose-covered arbors, stone benches with seats of thyme, cement fantasies imitating tree trunks, even old park benches. Choose a seat that pleases you

This rustic twig bench, **RIGHT**, was constructed to fit between two trees. The unusual construction provides seating on both sides.

and is compatible with the garden, then put it in a shady corner, set it at the edge of the herb garden with its legs entwined by mint or thyme, or place it at the curve of a path where you can enjoy the view in both directions.

Furniture in the subtle colorations of natural materials fits unobtrusively into any garden setting and is especially good for small spaces where no element should overpower the eye. Metal and wood furniture is frequently painted, most traditionally in dark green or black, colors that blend seamlessly into the background. White stands out against the natural green of the garden and will focus attention on the seat, although its eye-catching quality diminishes if there are other white elements in the garden.

Another good basic color for garden seating is a soft gray-blue that harmonizes with stone. Pale greens and blues with a greenish cast are an offbeat but attractive alternative when used sparingly.

ABOVE: Elizabeth Rocchia made her version of an English garden seat by combining a bench and trompe l'oeil painting on the side of a garden shed. LEFT: On an English terrace, traditional wooden chairs are painted dark green. A curved stone bench, BELOW, graces the gardens at Jenkyn Place in England.

Audrey Julian and her husband, Doug, live in a handsome rural Pennsylvania building that started life as a general store in 1758 and has operated continuously as a retail establishment ever since. When Audrey first saw the building, she immediately envisioned herb gardens in place of the old tires and other trash that had accumulated under the house's ancient

A STORE OF herbs

lilac bushes; she knew she'd found the perfect spot for her family as well as her shop specializing in American country gifts and antiques.

Soon after moving in, Doug and their son, Chris, tackled the job of carting away fifty years' worth of accumulated trash and overgrown bushes. Meanwhile, Audrey was planning her first garden, a freestanding oval in the middle of the lawn where lilac bushes had once grown. After Audrey plotted the shape on paper, Chris helped her dig the garden and set in an edging made of stones salvaged from an old barn that once stood on the property. Audrey also traversed the oval with stone paths to make caring for and picking the herbs easier.

Over the years Audrey has refined the garden, moving plants from one part of the garden to another for a more visually pleasing whole or if something gets too big for the space. Since the Julians spend two or three weeks in Maine each summer, low-maintenance herbs such as thyme and sage have usurped much of the space; and because her time is at a premium, Audrey favors perennials such as pinks and dusty

PRECEDING PAGES: An old twig bench nestles among the herbs in the oval herb garden. To compensate for the slope of the land, the stone edging becomes a retaining wall on the lower side. RIGHT: Audrey makes her own herb markers from shims used for cedar roofing. THIS PAGE, LEFT: The main reason for siting the garden in the middle of the lawn was to ensure it received enough sun despite the many trees on the property. The resulting herbal island, LEFT, is filled with an assortment of culinary favorites such as chives and thyme and decorative plants like lamb's ears and santolina. A few perennial geraniums add color. On sunny days Audrey often hangs a colorful

quilt over a washline suspended, colonial-style, on tripods of young saplings. An old painted wheelbarrow doubles as a planter for geraniums. Audrey uses baskets of fresh flowers and herbs, BELOW, to decorate her garden.

miller over annuals and welcomes self-seeding herbs such as calendula and foxglove. Another time-saver is the system she has devised to eliminate weeding: three times a season, the gardens are mulched with minichips, which discourage unwanted growth while keeping the beds looking well-tended.

Once the oval garden was established, Audrey began tucking in herbs wherever she could find space, adding a small garden against the house and more in front of the house. There, yarrow and artemisia thrive, serving the dual purpose of landscaping and yielding a bountiful harvest for Audrey to dry. She ties them into bunches to hang from the beams and

peg racks in the store and the kitchen, and uses them in the handsome wreaths and swags she creates for the shop. More herbs grow in the corner next to the porch and in attractive pots and barrels.

Since Audrey has a talent for decorating, it's not surprising that she has decorated the garden, too, adding to its charm and personality. Authentic bee skeps nestle among the herbs, along with such diverse pieces as terra-cotta bunnies, old weather vanes, and handcrafted signs. Whirligigs perch on stumps and old tools and baskets are displayed on the wall behind the fenced garden. The birdhouses she's collected, many of them created by leading American folk artists, tower above the gardens on poles or sit among the herbs. Benches scattered about invite visitors to relax and enjoy the sights and scents just as Audrey does. "Just looking at my herbs gives me such pleasure," she says with a smile.

LEFT: An old tree stump surrounded by herbs and flowers makes a perfect perch for a birdhouse. **ABOVE:** Yarrow grows abundantly by the front door. **OPPOSITE:** The plan of the small garden outside the kitchen door is based on a diamond shape and defined by brick paths. Raised beds keep the garden neat and a low picket fence sets the boundaries without blocking the view.

From the outside there is little to distinguish Serge Lesné's house from the others lining the street in this small city in Brittany. But once you step through the front door into the pristine house filled with *objets* and furniture he has selectively collected over the years, glass doors at the back provide a pleasing view of the arresting town house garden. "It's a secret," he says. "You can't see it from the street." This is Serge's first garden, designed and planted in

A TOWN HOUSE garden

PRECEDING PAGES: Like the garden paths, the sunken "courtyard" that leads to the entry, LEFT, is paved with old stones, but to make the space seem larger, it is punctuated by a deep green living carpet of baby's tears; pennyroyal, thyme, or clipped chamomile would serve as well. RIGHT: A narrow path leads through the garden down some steps to the courtyard of the old washhouse and garage at the back. Serge is in the process of converting them to a guest-house. Clever planting isolates the two seating areas. THIS PAGE: The incredible blue of the garden furniture, a harmonious accent to the greenery and stone, was copied from the furniture in his grandmother's garden. In a niche, an urn holds a collection of stones instead of a plant and the sheen of a mercury ball in a metal plant stand lights up the corner. Serge's abiding love for old stone, coupled with his deft way of using decorative accessories are what really set this garden apart.

conjunction with landscape architect Timothy Vaughan. "The most important part of a garden is the plan," he says. "Without it you make mistakes."

Serge had two prerequisites for his garden: The first was that it be pretty and give him pleasure without too much work. The combination of herbs and flowers, selected not only for color and suitability to the climate but also for ease of care, was densely planted to eliminate much of the weeding problem. The flowering trees need to be trimmed only once a year to maintain their shapeliness and keep their size under control.

The second requirement was that old stones be incorporated in the patio and paths. Smooth oval stones picked up on walks share space with formal stone statuary and round granite balls that once graced the posts of a mansion's gateway. Small potted box plants echo this spherical shape and help soften the expanse of stone in the two seating areas. "I've decorated the garden like a room," says Serge.

ABOVE: A stone basin filled with smooth stones collected on trips suggests a large egg-filled bird's nest. **BELOW:** Varicolored foliage creates a handsome background for items from Serge's collection of stone objects. The entrance to the patio is marked with varied size balls of regular and golden box and enclosed by shrubs to create the feeling of a separate room, **RIGHT,** where Serge often relaxes.

imothy went to Australia in his teens as an adventure; there he was overwhelmed by the country's vegetation, and discovered his affinity for plants. "The love of gardening is in you or it's not," he says. Back in England, he honed his craft at the prestigious English garden schools at Wisley and Kew Gardens, and he later moved to the coast of Brittany. Here, with his wife, Isabel, a painter and avid gardener, he established a nursery in 1982, eventually buying a wonderful old stone house nearby at the edge of the English Channel. Since then, any time that can be spared from the nursery has been spent on the house and garden.

Building a garden with structure and a long-term vision has been the strength of the great English landscape architects, and Timothy scoffs at the notion that garden structure has become antiquated. His garden, strictly of this time and place, is splendid proof of the importance of historic foundations. "The design of this garden, defined with pavers and trees, can last for hundreds of years," he claims. "It will be beautiful for my children even if they don't want flowers."

The garden was planned and planted during the restoration of the house, and is clearly visible through the windows because "the garden is a continuation of the house," says Timothy. Since the house is on a steep site, the land had to be bulldozed and terraced to accommodate his plans. "The garden was not designed on paper. I design directly in the earth, defining the design with bamboo stakes and string," he says. Installed over a period of time, the enormous garden is actually a series of smaller

PRECEDING PAGES: Warm yellows and oranges from such plants as calendula, lilies, daisies, and yarrow predominate in this section of the garden, LEFT. The courtyard garden is entered through a wooden door, RIGHT. Moss growing between the pavers imbues the path with a sense of history. THIS PAGE, LEFT: A grass path is both more practical and decorative when edged and inlaid with diamond-shaped steps of pavers. ABOVE: Containers mixing the variegated foliage of such plants as tricolor sage and licorice plant (*Helichrysum petiolatum*) with the feathery foliage of golden marguerite daisies (*Anthemis*) and the large leaves of a scented geranium would enhance the garden even without their flowers. OPPOSITE: Giant mounds of cerise perennial geraniums lead the eye along the path to the house. Throughout the garden color is rampant but under control, as one family of color ends before another begins.

gardens arranged along an axis that climbs the terraced hill.

Clusters of potted plants play an important part in his garden, too, and Timothy is a master of turning them into arresting still lifes, juxtaposing colors and textures. He enjoys this kind of planting because it allows him to mix colors that might not work in a garden, and to use those plants whose short blooming period would leave a visual hole in the landscape. "You can indulge a whim of the moment, then change it during the season with ease," he says. "There is really no limit except your imagination and the availability of plants. Even when you're living with only a small terrace, you can have an herb garden in pots."

PRECEDING PAGES: In the courtyard garden pavers have been laid in a handsome circular pattern. Although many of the plants here grow up through the pavers, additional greenery and color come from a collection of well-planted containers. THIS PAGE: The pattern of the pavers used inside the house, LEFT, reflects that of the garden. RIGHT: Aromatic foliage plants such as santolina and rosemary are used throughout the garden because they're evergreen, they withstand the salt winds and drought, can be clipped into shapes, and have pretty flowers. OPPOSITE: A circular garden near the house, planted in a tapestry of blue agapanthus, pink brachycome and convolvulus mauritanicus, greens, and gray cineraria with small accents of yellow kniphofia, is based on a 16th-century plunge pool. Another view of the courtyard, BELOW, where a stand of bronze fennel contrasts handsomely with the colorful flowers.

At Jenkyn Place in Hampshire, England, a massive old terra-cotta oil jar, **ABOVE**, is used as a planter, as is a decorative lead container, **BELOW**. Like cement, lead is nearly indestructible, but both are heavy and not easily portable. Fiberglass look-alikes are an alternative.

CONTAINER GARDENING

Growing herbs in containers can be a necessity if you are short on space, but even in a big garden, pots of herbs add a special charm. Use a handsome pot to draw attention to a pool or a pretty spot on a path; cluster several pots together to make a "bouquet" on a deck or terrace; welcome guests with a parade of pots up the front steps; put a pot of flowering plants in a corner where perennial blossoms have faded; or fill one with a special plant like a topiary that requires extra care or has to be brought in for the winter.

ABOVE RIGHT: An old dog cart holds pots of Mexican sage in my garden. **RIGHT:** In the garden behind his shop in Bruges, Belgium, floral designer Carl Vandermoere gardens primarily in pots.

ABOVE: Boxwood spheres in fluted terra-cotta pots enhance the steps of a house. In Old Salem, North Carolina, an old millstone embedded in stone acts as a planter for mint, RIGHT. Unused clay pots are neatly stacked to provide a decorative touch at Bourton House in Gloucestershire, BELOW. Although terra-cotta allows roots to breathe freely, it also permits water to evaporate rapidly, requiring more frequent watering.

TOP: Marge Haller grows a mini garden of scented geraniums, thyme, and sage in a sturdy wooden container. ABOVE: Elsewhere in her Ohio garden she collects a variety of scented geraniums on a plant stand.

At Pound House catnip blooms in the top of a stone wall, RIGHT. Most plants can be grown in a container if roots have ample room and adequate drainage, and if ample nourishment is provided.

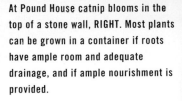

There are a few simple rules for successful container gardening. First, select a container big enough to give the roots of the plants ample room to grow. Second, make sure the plant has adequate drainage, drilling more drainage holes in the bottom if necessary. If the container has no drainage or is very large, put a layer of perlite or plastic peanuts in the bottom third of the pot, add some powdered charcoal to keep the soil sweet, and cover this with a piece of fine screening. Next, add premoistened commercial potting soil or your own mixture made from one-third perlite or builder's sand, one-third topsoil, and one-third sphagnum moss. Ordinary garden soil is too heavy for container growing.

Arrange the plants in your container, placing the tallest ones in the center and creeping or hanging plants at the out-

ABOVE LEFT: Pansies and cascading ivy are complementary partners in this graceful planting. **LEFT:** Lemon-scented geranium flourishes in a terra-cotta pot on the terrace at Timothy Vaughan's house. **TOP RIGHT:** Rosemary thrives in an old half-barrel container surrounded by mint in this Ohio garden. **ABOVE:** Hibiscus topiaries in handsome terra-cotta pots provide easily portable color and decor on Bernard Perris's Provençal terrace.

LEFT: Audrey Julian turns an old Coca-Cola crate perched on a stump into a miniature garden by planting it with a variety of herbs such as sage, chives, and thyme. Daisies add a spot of color. RIGHT: Geraniums, scented or plain, make handsome pot plants indoors and out. BELOW: Pansies thrive in an old horse trough. BOTTOM: Licorice plant and geraniums combine handsomely in this cement planter at Folly Farm, in Berkshire, England.

side where they will trail over the edge of the pot. Add more soil around the plants and water them in gently. Feed the plants with a 50 percent solution of organic fertilizer such as fish emulsion every other week. During the warmest part of the summer, hot air and sun will dry the soil out quickly, so water the plants daily if not twice a day. To check whether it's time to water, stick your finger 1 to 2 inches into the soil. If it is dry, water. Mixing some polymer granules into the soil might be advisable if the plants are going to be in a very hot, windy spot; these granules retain water without making the soil so soggy that roots will rot.

Almost any herb can be grown successfully in a pot, but it is wise to avoid those with long taproots such as angelica, dill, and fennel. Invasive herbs such as mint must also be approached with caution and their roots contained. One solution is to set them in the container in a pot whose bottom has been removed.

In planning your pot, consider harmonizing colors and contrasting leaf textures, or concentrate on a specific category of herbs. For example, plant a French kitchen garden of sorrel, chervil, thyme, savory, chives, and marjoram, and if the container is big enough, place a small bay tree in the center. Or make a potted fragrance garden by mixing the contrasting foliage of lavender, lemon verbena, scented geraniums, santolina, and rosemary. Or just fill the entire pot with a glorious array of pansies or poppies.

children, who cut the owner's lawn, reported that he had doused it with kerosene and was about to destroy it, she rushed over to convince him to sell her the little building along with an acre of land. The deal was finalized with 25¢ and a handshake.

She planned to use the cottage as a workroom where she could make wreaths and other herbal decorations without wreaking havoc on her house and garden. However, neighbors were so fascinated by the restoration and garden that she unexpectedly found herself proprietor of The Summer House selling herb plants and decorations.

Oris uses the garden to demonstrate her rather casual approach to herbs. "The average person gets frustrated with a manicured look," she says. Beginning gardeners are warned not to buy an enormous number of plants. "It's better to start with just five or ten," she advises, "and learn as much about them as you can. And I also think you should grow things that are fun, like lady's mantle. The pleated leaf is so different and it's so pretty with that little dewdrop in the morning."

Unfortunately, sometimes a plant that looks appealing in a friend's garden, or at the nursery, turns out to be problem. "My first perilla came from a friend's driveway in Connecticut. That should have been a clue as to how noxious it was," she says. After it started taking over the garden, it was a chore to eradicate. "Mugwort is another invader," she notes. "Eventually I had to sift the garden soil to get rid of all the bits of runners." These plants should be planted where they can run wild, or the roots must be contained.

Though demanding, "gardening is the best therapy," says Oris. "I enjoy working among the herbs, pulling weeds. And when the snow blows, I like to look at my dried wreaths and bouquets. They let you share the joys of gardening all year long."

PRECEDING PAGES: Since the house, LEFT, rests on a glacial knoll with good drainage and the lower land, once a horse pasture, is rich in nutrients, the soil for the garden needed very little work. RIGHT: One of her son Kerry Hippensteel's dapper scarecrows stands amid a cluster of black-eyed Susans. THIS PAGE: On the advice of a friend, Oris waited six months before putting in the paths, ABOVE, allowing visitors to instinctively establish the most logical routes through the riotous display of herbs and flowers. For water plants, a pond with a little bridge was installed near the house, RIGHT. The garden was planned to highlight differences in texture and color. Scented geraniums, for example, are planted near delicate gray-leafed French lavender, large furry lamb's ears near the tiny, smooth-leafed thyme.

What could be more appealing in the garden than water? Whether it's a little brook meandering through a country garden, the tinkling spray of a fountain in a formal setting, or simply a small birdbath sitting amid masses of lavender, there is something infinitely calming and relaxing about water. It adds an extra dimension of pleasure to the garden, and in hot weather even the smallest amount manages to make the day seem cooler.

WATER

Jane Rivkin's decorative birdbath is almost hidden by catnip and lavender plants, **ABOVE. BELOW:** In Ohio Mary Flegle nestled an old stone trough among her herbs and filled it with water.

Carol Meyer finds that lamb's ears and thyme work well as rock plants around her pond, **ABOVE.** Marnie Diltz used stone to create a circular pond and herb garden, **LEFT.**

Water can be part of any garden, but it should be in harmony with the setting. Those lucky enough to have a brook running through their country garden need only plant the banks with watercress, marsh marigold, and other water-loving plants. Those without a natural water source might install a little pond. Since water naturally pools where the land is lowest, place the pond at a low point in the garden or at least on flat land. To build a small pond, excavate the space and line it with sand. Then either sink a preformed rigid plastic form, available at most garden centers, or line the space with a sheet of heavy plastic, holding the edges down with pins and rocks. Whichever method you use, cover the edges of your "pond" with stones and plant around them.

A more structured garden benefits from a reflecting pool or lily pond in a geometric shape best made from poured con-

ABOVE: Linda Barksdale's northwest garden plan takes advantage of the natural shoreline. LEFT: Wallace Huntington created a water feature in his Oregon garden by placing a custom-made shallow metal tray top on an old well. Jean Mus used inverted roof tiles, RIGHT, to guide a stream of water downhill to a Provençal stone basin. His Provençal fountain, BELOW LEFT, was cleverly constructed from a stone wall and an old stone basin. Nasturtiums and poppies grow in the rocks around Carol Meyer's pool in the Northwest, BELOW.

AN artist's vision
IN PROVENCE

"A house without a garden is like a woman without clothes," says Dominique Lafourcade, a designer for a leading French porcelain manufacturer. For the past five years, she has spent much of her time "dressing" her reno-vated farmhouse and other beautiful old Provençal houses that her husband, Bruno, an architect, has restored.

PRECEDING PAGES: An old sheep shelter that stood in front of the house was demolished to open up the view, then replaced with a pool that feeds into the canal, LEFT. The decorative stone balls were made by a local stonecutter. The terrace in front of the house is lined with neatly trimmed box in traditional glazed pots from Anduze, RIGHT. THIS PAGE: In the blue garden, mounds of lamb's ears and santolina spill out over the path, OPPOSITE. The eye-pleasing effect of the multitudes of green and the various shapes and sizes are the result of careful planning. Beds of lavender and cypress trees grow on either side of the canal, LEFT. BELOW: A wisteria-covered arbor runs along one side of the garden from the herb garden to the "green room." It is repeated on the opposite side.

A strong believer in respecting the environment, Dominique feels that "the plants in a garden shouldn't be an aberration. Don't plant those that need a lot of water where there is no water. You have to consider the climate, the winds." For this reason, she concentrates on plants native to Provence, such as bay laurel, cypress, lavender, sage, thyme, rosemary, and lamb's ears.

The Lafourcades' garden is a stunning example of Dominique's precise planning. Her inspiration comes from visiting gardens and perusing garden books. "Looking is the best gardening school," she insists. She will often make several plans for the same garden and choose the best. "The first step is the structure, walls," she says. "You have to consider the views you will see from the house and figure out how to hide what isn't pretty." She looks upon the garden as a continuation of the house and demands that it have an architectural perspective as well. Her garden's plan alternates open and closed spaces. Some areas aren't visible from the house, sav-

ing their enchantment for those who walk through the garden.

Whenever possible, Dominique, inspired by gardens she has visited in Italy where the "climate and vegetation are similar to those of Provence," introduces a water element to the garden. The long canal that flows from the pool in front of her house to a pump at the far end was designed to elongate the perspective, but is also symbolic of the irrigation canals that once provided water for the countryside.

garden PLANS

Whether you want a traditional garden based on symmetrically divided geometric spaces or a less classic adaptation that allows for personal preference or the shape of an existing site, it is imperative to start with a plan. Begin by drawing the exact outside measurements of the finished garden on graph paper, allowing 1 or 2 feet per square. Next, divide the interior space; the arrangement can be as simple as four squares or as complex as an intricate knot. Although straight lines are easiest to work with, a mixture of straight and curved lines is often more interesting.

Once the design is drawn to scale on graph paper—or on one of the new computer programs—transfer the layout to the proposed site. Start at one corner of the garden and measure carefully, driving stakes or plant supports at what will be the corner of each separate space. Then connect the appropriate stakes with string to define the outline of the beds. If the plan includes a circle or the arc of a circle, drive a stake where the center of the circle would be located. Attach a piece of string the length of the circle's radius. Grasp the outer end and a chalker or a can of surveyor's spray paint and, using the string as a guide, describe a circle around the stake. Once the garden is completely laid out, remove any sod and prepare the soil well. Since many herbs are perennials, it is especially important to start with friable, nutritionally balanced soil.

Here are a few plans to use for inspiration. Some are loosely based on gardens in this book, others on classic garden designs or decorative motifs. Adapt them to reflect the available space in your garden and plant them formally or informally according to your own personal taste and vision.

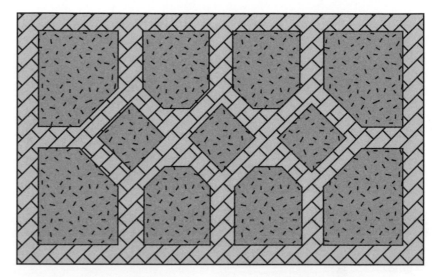

This plan was taken from Ryan Gainey's charming potager where the beds are edged with herbs like nasturtiums, parsley, and thyme. It would work equally well for herbs and flowers. Substituting boxwood or germander hedges for the herbal edgings would add a note of formality. Enclosing the entire garden with a wall, fence, or hedge would make it even more striking.

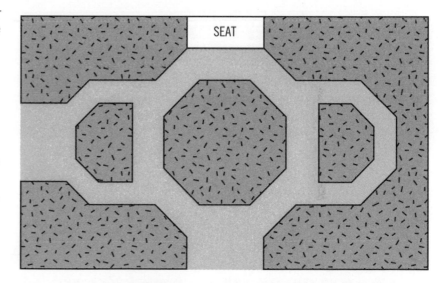

This is a rather formal garden layout that would lend itself to being enclosed with a tall hedge or wall while the beds were neatly edged with low herbal hedges or brick. The seat could be under a rose-covered arbor; arbors or gates might also define the two entrances.

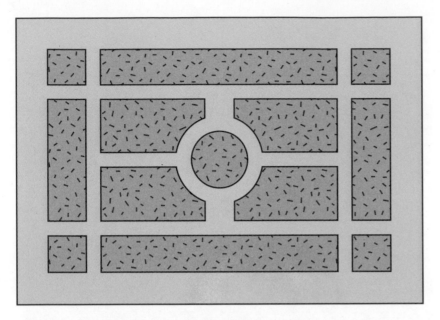

This garden plan was inspired by one at Westbury Court in Gloucestershire, England. Measurements could be changed to make it a square or the pattern could be repeated for a larger garden. For a very formal feeling, plant topiaries in each corner.

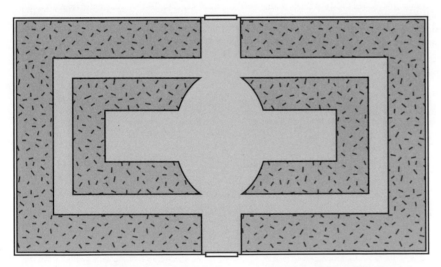

Inspired by Jeanne Marston's Pennsylvania garden, this is a good layout for a large, free-standing space. The two sections could be shortened to fit a smaller area. The beds are easily accessible, and the oval space in the center would welcome more planting and/or a decorative element such as a sundial. The entire garden would look best enclosed by a fence with arbors at each entrance.

The very precise geometric plan, ABOVE, lends itself to equally precise planting. This would be an excellent choice for a potager or a traditional herb garden. An herbal hedge would define the outer perimeter nicely. OPPOSITE: This garden design was inspired by the wonderful potager at Villandry in France. You can use one section on its own or arrange four sections to make a squarer layout. Edge each section in one herb or use raised beds to articulate the design. In this layout the circle could be a small pool or a birdbath or sundial surrounded by herbs.

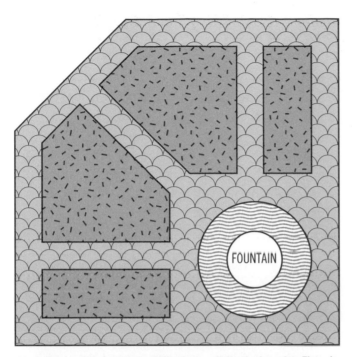

This design is taken from Kathy Collins's Napa Valley herb garden. There is a small fountain in the center of the circular pond, but this could be replaced by a sundial or birdbath surrounded by herbs.

This knot garden design is taken from Elaine Kheene's northwest garden. The outer square, the outline of the petals, and the circle should be planted with different herbs, such as gray santolina, box, hyssop, or rosemary, where the contrast in color and foliage will accentuate the pattern. Where the petals intersect, arrange the plants so it appears as if they intertwine.

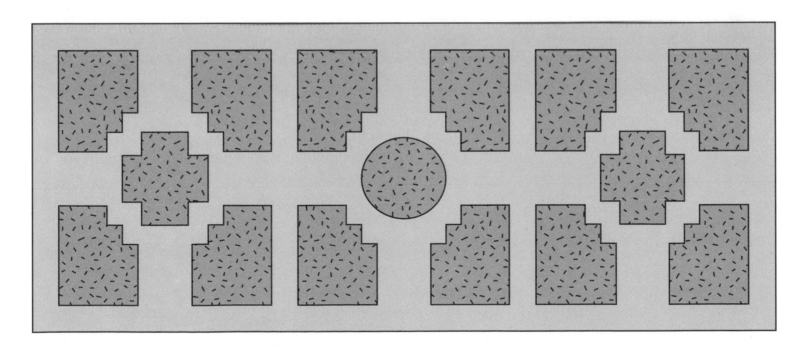

A List of POPULAR HERBS

The following chart lists more than seventy-five of the most popular herbs, their cultural requirements, and suggestions on how to use them in and out of the garden. If you desperately want to grow a favorite plant but your garden does not quite seem to meet its cultural needs, try it anyway: Most gardens have spots that are especially warm or cool where that particular plant just might work.

Select plans appropriate to your zone (see map, page 260), but use common sense, too. Remember, for example, a plant that thrives in full sun in cooler climates may survive under a hot southern sun but perform better with a little shade. Only through experimentation in your garden can you know for sure how it will fare; the same plant can do poorly in one part of a garden and grow like a weed one hundred feet away. Use this chart as a guide to which plants should grow successfully in your area, then add to your knowledge by visiting local nurseries and gardens.

NAME	ZONE	LIGHT	TYPE	HEIGHT	SOIL	PROPAGATION	USES	COMMENTS
Alkanet (*Anchusa*)	3	S	P	3'–4'	Rich, well-drained	Division, self-seeds	Dye	Beautiful deep blue flowers mid to back of border in late spring. Several varieties, with *A. Dropmore* being the tallest.
Angelica (*Angelica Archangelica*)	3	S, PS	B	4–8	Moist, humus, alkaline	Seed, self-seeds	Culinary, medicinal, dye, cosmetics, liqueurs	Back of the border, large greenish-white globe-shaped flowers, large-toothed leaves. Cut flowers before seeds form to make plant act like a perennial.
Anise (*Pimpinella Anisum*)		S	A	2'	Light, dry, well-drained	Seed, self-sows	Culinary, medicinal, cosmetic	Small umbels of creamy white flowers, feathery leaves. Seeds have a distinct licorice flavor.
Anise Hyssop (*Agastache Foeniculum*)	5	S, PS	P	40"	Well-drained, moderately rich sandy loam	Seed, cuttings, root division, self-seeds	Culinary, potpourri	Long-lasting purple spires look good in groups in border; attracts bees and butterflies. Tastes of both mint and anise.
Baptisia (*Baptisia australis*)	3	S, PS	P	3'–4'	Even moisture, lime-free	Seed, division, self-seeds	Seed pods for decoration, ornamental	Spires of deep blue flowers. Light airy foliage and seed pods are handsome after flowers are finished.
Basil (*Ocimum Basilicum*)		S	A	2'–3'	Rich, moist, well-drained	Seed	Culinary, fragrance	The traditional culinary herb. Other varieties range from small mounds of tiny green leaves for edging, to taller ruffled varieties. Flavors from cinnamon to lemon. Green- and red-leafed varieties. Kitchen garden.
Bay (*Laurus nobilis*)	8	S	P	5'–10' in a pot; 40'–60' outdoors	Moderately rich, good drainage	Cuttings	Culinary, decorative	Can be grown as a tub plant in cool climates; as a standard; or as a tree or hedge in warm areas.
Bergamot (*Monarda didyma*)	3	S, PS	P	2'–4'	Moist, humusy	Division, spreads by roots	Culinary, decorative, arrangements, potpourri	Wonderful shaggy edible flowers in shades of pink, red, violet, white. Minty leaves. Mildly invasive.
Borage (*Borago officinalis*)		S	A	3'	Light, dry to normal	Seed, self-seeds	Culinary	Beautiful bright blue edible flowers, large rough grayish leaves. Can be floppy.
Boxwood (*Buxus sempervirens*)	6	S, PS	P	2'–10'	Rich, humusy, moist	Cuttings	Decorative	Evergreen shiny, bright green leaves. Dwarf variety for edging and knot gardens. Good for topiary. *B. microphylla* var. *koreana* is better for cold climates

ind

NAME	ZONE	LIGHT	TYPE	HEIGHT	SOIL	PROPAGATION	USES	COMMENTS
Butterfly Weed (*Asclepias tuberosa*)	3	S	P	15"–36"	Well-drained, sandy	Seed or division	Decorative, dye	Clusters of bright orange flowers at the top of the stalk add color to the garden; attracts butterflies.
Calamint (*Calamintha nepetoides*)	5	S	P	18"	Average soil, well drained	Cuttings, self-seeds	Tea, medicinal	Fragrant leaves, tiny pink-white flowers. Can be used in borders, rock gardens.
Calendula (*Calendula officinalis*)		S, PS	A	18"–24"	Fertile, well-drained	Seed, self-seeds	Culinary, medicinal, cosmetic, arrangements	Pale yellow to deep orange daisylike flowers.
Caraway (*Carum Carvi*)	3, 4	S	B	15"–30"	Well-drained	Seed, self-seeds	Culinary	Umbels of white flowers, finely cut leaves. Primarily grown for flavorful seeds.
Catnip/Catmint (*Nepeta* ssp.)	3	S, PS	P	15"–3'	Average, sandy, well-drained	Cuttings, division, self-seeds	Scent, tea, baths, medicinal	Heart-shaped gray leaves, spires of purple or white flowers. Good edging plant. Several varieties.
Chamomile, Roman (*Chamaemelum nobile*)		S, PS	P	9"	Light, dry	Seed, divisions	Tea, cosmetics	Good ground cover. Lacy foliage, tiny white daisy-like flowers, apple scent.
Chervil (*Anthriscus cerefolium*)		PS	A or B	2'	Normal, moist, humusy	Seed, self-sows	Culinary	Small umbels of white flowers, deeply cut leaves. Sow every 2 weeks.
Chives (*Allium Schoenoprasum*)	3	S	P	15"–24"	Moist, fertile, well-drained	By seed or division, self-seeds	Culinary, flowers in dried arrangements	Can be used as edging plant, reddish-purple blossoms.
Clary Sage (*Salvia Sclarea*)	5	S	B/P	3'–5'	Good drainage, sandy loam	Self-sows	Medicinal, culinary, cosmetics	Stalks of pale blue, white, or pink flowers look pretty in a border. Leaves make good fritters; flowers edible.
Comfrey (*Symphytum officinale*)		S, PS	P	3'–5'	Moist, rich	Division	Cosmetic, medicinal. May be dangerous.	Handsome sprays of pink flowers, large dark-green leaves.
Coneflower (*Echinacea purpurea*)	3	S, PS	P	24"–40"	Ordinary, well-drained	Division, seed	Medicinal, flower arrangements, ornamental	Masses of pale purple daisylike flowers centered on an orange cone. Good toward back of border or in informal gardens.
Coriander (*Coriandrum sativum*)		S, PS	A	12"–18"	Medium, well-drained	Seed, self-seeds	Culinary	Plant every two weeks for ongoing supply. Important in Asian, Mexican, and Middle Eastern cooking. Kitchen garden.
Costmary (*Chrysanthemum Balsamita*)	4	S, PS	P	3'–4'	Any	Division, spreads by roots	Scent, minor culinary, cosmetic	Fairly invasive. Yellow button flowers, large serrated leaves. Becomes straggly after flowering if not cut back.
Curry Plant (*Helichrysum angustifolium*)	9	S	P	12"–15"	Average, dry	Seed	Decorative	Small yellow flowers above narrow gray leaves. Smells like curry but is not used in the kitchen. Flowers dry well. Treat as an annual.
Dill (*Anethum graveolens*)		S	A	3'–4'	Good, moist	Seed, self-seeds	Culinary, flower arrangements	Large umbels of yellow flowers, feathery foliage. Grown for seed as well as greenery.
Elderberry (*Sambucus* spp. *canadensis*)	4	S, PS	P	4'–10'	Moist, rich	Cuttings, suckers	Culinary, cosmetic	Large umbels of creamy white edible flowers followed by masses of dark purple berries. Spreads.
Elecampane (*Inula Helenium*)	3	SH, PS	P	4'–6'	Moist, well-drained heavy soil	Seed, division	Medicinal, liqueurs	Yellow daisylike flowers on tall stems with large hairy leaves. Blooms most of summer.

10

To plant su
your garde
for your cli
zones, plar
excessively
Remember
rainfall, ligl

Living cl
effect on o
warmer zor
than the ne
Northwest
the other h